CW00431836

# APPLE FIRE

*Drawing:* KIT SWINDALE, *12*

# Apple Fire

## THE HALESWORTH MIDDLE SCHOOL ANTHOLOGY

EDITED BY

## Jill Pirrie

WITH A FOREWORD BY

## Edward Blishen

BLOODAXE BOOKS

Introduction and selection © Jill Pirrie 1993
Foreword © Edward Blishen 1993

Copyright of poems and drawings rests
with the authors as acknowledged on each page.

ISBN: 1 85224 206 X

First published 1993 by
Bloodaxe Books Ltd,
P.O. Box 1SN,
Newcastle upon Tyne NE99 1SN.

Bloodaxe Books Ltd acknowledges
the financial assistance of Northern Arts.

LEGAL NOTICE

All rights reserved. No part of this book may be
reproduced, stored in a retrieval system, or
transmitted in any form, or by any means, electronic,
mechanical, photocopying, recording or otherwise,
without prior written permission from Bloodaxe Books Ltd.

Requests to publish work from this book
must be sent to Bloodaxe Books Ltd.

ARTWORK

Special thanks are due to Laurie Shepherd,
art teacher at Halesworth Middle School, and to his pupils,
for their help with this anthology.  J.P.

Cover printing by J. Thomson Colour Printers Ltd, Glasgow.

Printed in Great Britain by
The Alden Press, Osney Mead, Oxford.

*For the children*
*of Halesworth Middle School,*
*past and present.*

LOUISE DESBOROUGH, *13*

# Acknowledgements

*W.H. Smith Young Writers Competition:*
1987 (published in *Young Words*, Pan Macmillan, 1988): SPECIAL AWARD: Caroline English 'Chicken Lucky' and 'The Fly'. MAJOR AWARD: Emma Graves: 'Flaming June'; Helen Walkey: 'Starling'; Thea Smiley: 'The Truth of a Bluebottle'. RUNNER-UP AWARD: Matthew Line: 'Winter'; Mark Clarke: 'Grandad'; Robert Adcock: 'The Old Lady'; Helen Ward: 'The Grasshopper'; Marie Fenn: 'The Thought Cat'.
1988 (*Young Words*, Pan Macmillan, 1989): MAJOR AWARD: Thea Smiley: 'Reflection'; Lara Mair: 'Sailing with Reflection'; Clifford Black: 'Ants', 'Reflections' and 'The Ford'; Hilary Foster: 'The Truth of a Bullfinch'. RUNNER-UP AWARD: Robert Adcock: 'Nicholas' and 'Snail'; Helen Ward: 'The Autumn Snail'; Scott Spindler: 'The Shimmering Books'; Kirsty Butcher: 'The Cow'; Denise Revell: 'The Silent Cowshed'; Oliver Mac-Donald: 'Winter Churchyard'; Heidi Masters: 'The Journey'.
1989 (*Young Words*, Pan Macmillan, 1990): MAJOR AWARD: Stephen Gardam: 'Cat'. RUNNER-UP AWARD: Rhys Harper: 'Truth of the Cockerel' and 'The Bluebottle'; Richard Munnings: 'Moth'; Emma Walkey: 'The Christmas Spider'.
1990 (*Young Words*, Pan Macmillan, 1991): SPECIAL AWARD: Stephen Gardam: 'Dunwich', 'The Time of Day' and 'Fox'. MAJOR AWARD: Michelle Barnes: 'The Tadpole Is…' and 'The Peacock'; Hannah Edwards: 'The Pheasant' and 'Robin'; Emma Buckingham: 'The Winter Seashore'; Marnie Smith: 'Mastitis'; Gavin Goodwin: 'The Winter Hare'; Joanna Tyler: 'The Maternity Ward'. RUNNER-UP AWARD: Edward Line: 'Grandad'.
1991 (*Inky Foot*, Pan Macmillan, 1992): MAJOR AWARD: Sara Worts: 'Conkers' and 'Astronaut'; Emma Walkey: 'Snapdragon'; William Mair: '*Shelter Scene: Bunks and Sleepers*'. RUNNER-UP AWARD: Gemma White: '*Ennui*' and 'Reflections'; Jessica Brown: 'Fossil', 'Seal' and 'Rockpool Reflections'; James Noble: 'American Cat in London'; Suzanne Alderton: 'The Dream of the Fisherman'; Paul Batley: 'The Marsh Man'.
*Cadburys National Exhibition of Children's Art (Poetry Section):*
Published in the Cadbury Books of Children's Poetry:
1988: *The Sixth Book:* Lara Mair: 'She Called It Her Robin' and 'At Dunwich' (ARTHUR LINES AWARD).
1990: *The Eighth Book:* Emma Buckingham: 'Birth' (SILVER MEDAL AWARD); Robert Filby: 'Red Squirrel'.
1991: *The Ninth Book:* Stephen Morris: 'First Day at Church'.
*Broadcast on BBC Radio 5:*
*Talking Poetry* (June 1991): Hannah Edwards: 'Creatures of the Classroom'; Sara Worts: 'Sports Day'; Niki Hurren: 'The Playground'.

# Contents

## 4. FARM, FIELD AND GARDEN
### (AND AN AMERICAN CAT IN LONDON)

## 5. DREAMS AND HAUNTINGS

# FOREWORD

In London annually a set of judges, chaired by Ted Hughes, grapple as best they can with an astonishment that does not lessen for becoming familiar. It is the astonishment of finding, and having found last year, and being sure one will find next year, that from a single school come poems, forty, fifty, sixty of them, sifted from many thousands received from schools all over the British Isles: and that these poems are of great quality, true poems, exciting in their phrasing, startling as a good poem must be, but never startling for the sake of it, all strongly individual, all clearly from the same stable. They are written by pupils of Jill Pirrie, who has said 'English teachers never work alone'. They are the work, indeed, of an extraordinary teacher *and* the young poets she calls into existence, liberates, in children who have in common only the fact that they are pupils of Halesworth Middle School. Unless there is something in the air of this corner of Suffolk that under encouragement makes ready poets of its natives – and that plainly is nonsense – then what is proved is that most children, certainly between the ages of ten and thirteen, are able (and, as it turns out, most seriously and unfussily eager) to make the response to experience that we recognise as poetry. But a feat of teacherly magic is required, of an obviously rare order.

Jill Pirrie has given her own account of the achievement, and does it again in her introduction to this anthology. But (and it is one of the facts of our imaginative lives of which she assists her children to be aware) there is a view from inside, and a view from outside: and I went once to Halesworth in pursuit of the latter. As an old teacher myself, I'm anxious to keep at bay, as I try to describe what I saw, the usual vocabulary in which teaching is discussed. One root of her beautiful power as a teacher, I'm certain, lies in her freedom from conventional pedagogy. I don't mean that she is any sort of conscious maverick. But she has invented for herself, out of a passion for originality that becomes the children's passion for it, the form that work in the classroom will take, the character of her own presence in the classroom, her relationship with the children and theirs with her: the pace at which they work, and the way in which their eagerness is tapped.

I suppose one has to start with that last. She knows how to cause children to be eager. And that, like everything else she does, lies in the work. They are eager because from the moment they enter the classroom they are at work, and because an atmosphere is created in which it is obvious to everyone present that the work is deep and worth doing, and leads to an extraordinary sense of well-being.

Jill Pirrie talks of peer expectation being as important as teacher expectation. The fact is that here is a room in which you cannot imagine the teacher ever saying, in whatever refined form, what some perfectly decent teachers commonly say: You have let me down, or You have done well by my teaching. In Jill Pirrie's classroom that is never the point. After sitting there for a memorable day during which the presence of an intruder was absorbed into the busyness, I could not explain how she made herself the plain mistress of the occasion without ever causing her power to dwarf or lessen the power of the children. But I guess it is a political matter, partly: her whole conduct, out of which theirs springs, makes it seem desirable to the children that they should have high expectations of each other, and that each should attempt to justify those expectations.

Add to this a curious and very robust delicacy in her. She does not thrust an observation at her children. As I felt it, what she did was to enfold them in it: it was hers, but it was instantly theirs. A great courtesy – but, as I say, robust. She simply and convincingly takes it that they are with her. I've never seen a teacher so close to those she's teaching, without reducing herself in any way. Her language is at times quite grand. It's one of the reasons for the success of her teaching, I think: that the children know she's giving herself as she is, not some teacherly simplification of herself. I was reminded of those marvellous lines of Lawrence's, in the poem he called 'The Best of School':

> I feel them cling and cleave to me
> As vines going eagerly up; they twine
> My life with other leaves, my time
> Is hidden in theirs, their thrills are mine.

Except that in Jill Pirrie's classroom you feel that it works both ways: the teacher's thrills are also theirs. It is an order of reciprocity I haven't encountered elsewhere. And a swiftness and attentiveness of it: nothing is spilled, because there's a constant readiness to receive.

*Nothing* priggish about it. They're too honestly busy for that. Their being country children, many from working backgrounds in which it would be daft not to be down-to-earth, may help in providing that 'robust commonsense' that Jill Pirrie points to as an essential ingredient of their work: but I would guess that this is a teacher who could just as well tap the commonsense in urban children. Another point about what I saw: she roots what she and the children do together in the plain – or fancy – facts of their experience. That's where the commonsense comes from. They may send their imaginations far beyond the daily scene, think of ghosts, or of looking down on the earth from space: but it's the need to note what's really felt, what might really be seen – the practicality of it – that is clung to even when, perhaps specially when, the aim has some touch of exaltation about it.

They form a guild whose business is the making of poetry, and the exchanges between them, provided by Jill Pirrie with a quite tense timetable, are craftsmen's exchanges. They struggle privately with a subject: switch urgently to swapping news of work in progress: return to privacy. It's all urgent, but easily urgent: all tense, yet relaxed. They'll switch again, to reading aloud completed or half-completed work, and discussing it. There's a floating of ideas and principles and perceptions and guesses and suggestions sometimes instantly withdrawn and replaced...about handling an image, finding the useable items in an experience, borrowing from one experience to enrich another. It's poet's talk, not a doubt about it. Theirs is a poetry of images, resemblances, connections. Audacities are admired. I said they didn't startle for the sake of it: what Jill Pirrie constantly says in the classroom, in one way or another, is that the seizing of attention is everything, and that attention can't be seized unless you discover what is fresh in your response, or locate the oddness there is in everything. Their alertness to this notion provides some of the tension there is in what they do. A feature of a lesson, if that's what it is, is the exorcising of cliché: a running labour, but sometimes attempted by giving attention, for a packed ten minutes or so, to a poem or story that demonstrably has no laziness or staleness in it.

Because what they create together is so unusual and stirring, and one wants to celebrate and insist on that, as well as to think about the extraordinary implications (for instance, how much of this can be copied, and what there is to copy), it's easy to make Jill Pirrie and her pupils sound like prodigies and paragons, which is exactly what they are not. I remember that classroom in terms of the 'state of concentration, dreamlike in its intensity' that Jill Pirrie says is her aim. I remember it rapt and unlazy as no other classroom I've ever been in. I remember realising that they'd all been infected, with complete success, with the habit of looking hard at what they saw, registering keenly what they felt, and finding words and images for sight and feeling (and clearly doing it all the time, and not just in the classroom), and that they'd very simply become intolerant of idleness of language. But the classroom was full of the usual human stuff. They rallied each other amusingly (though never with irrelevance to the matter in hand. The irrelevant had ruled itself out). The secret of it is not to be sought in the phenomenal. It *is* an astonishing achievement: but one thing certain about it is that it springs out of a very great diligence in the matter of being ordinary, everyday, plain observers of the world, plain recorders of what is observed.

The ultimate excitement of it is that, working with children who are like other children, and making poetry her medium (and no one should under-estimate the professional strength and courage required in doing that), Jill Pirrie has demonstrated that plain literacy is an infinitely larger affair than most of us ever allow it to be. You can aim to promote it through cautious banalities, anaemic exercises, dullnesses and smallnesses of every kind, believing that if you know one thing about those you teach it is that grandness is not for them: they are incapable of it and do not seek it. Jill Pirrie works on the perfectly opposite principle: and gives her children, by way of literacy, a fantastic measure of what makes a poet: and habits of language and outlook that must, for a lifetime, be grander than they would ever otherwise have been.

This happens to be a moment in the history of education in Britain when it is a particular joy to celebrate the achievement of a defiantly original teacher of English.

EDWARD BLISHEN

# INTRODUCTION

For many years the poetry written by the children of Halesworth Middle School has attracted attention and it is a particular pleasure to bring together a selection of some of the best work written lately. It is always difficult to account for quality in children's writing but W. Hart-Smith's words provide a starting point:

> Someone seeing me
> staring so fixedly
> at nothing
>
> might be excused
> for thinking me vague, abstracted,
>
> lost in introspection.
> No! I am awake, absorbed,
>
> just looking in a different direction.
>
> W. HART-SMITH (from 'Observation')

Here, Hart-Smith writes of the special wakefulness and attention to detail which is the mark of the poet:

> like this crack in sandstone
> perpetually wet with seepage.

Only when children achieve that relaxed intensity in which they are thrown on their own resources in an act of memory which returns them to their own narrow world are they freed to write well. Within their ordinary experience lies the impetus to write and it is the teacher's challenge to release this impetus in opportunities for 'just looking in a different direction'. The English teacher must provide new perspectives on the ordinary world. And this is a relentless quest for ideas.

In *The Language of the Night* Ursula LeGuin says:

> ...experience isn't something you go and *get* – it's a gift, and the only prerequisite for receiving it, is that you be open to it.

She uses as her illustration Emily and Charlotte Brontë within whose narrow world so many have been released into a new awareness which transcends time, place, and circumstance. LeGuin continues:

> From the time they were seven or eight years old, they wrote, and thought, and learned the landscape of their own being and how to describe it. They wrote with the imagination...They wrote from inside, from as deep inside as they could get by using all their strength and courage and intelligence.

The children in our classrooms have all this 'strength and courage and intelligence' and it is most particularly the business of the English teacher to harness such seriousness in those moments of reflective wakefulness that so often have all the appearance of abstraction. There is a moment in Alan Garner's 'Elidor' which embodies in story form the intensity of the creative artist's act of memory and makes it entirely accessible to children. Roland must make a door if he is to enter the Mound of Vandwy. To do this, he must remember the door he knows best. In a supreme act of concentration he sees:

> the blisters in the paint, and the brass flap with 'Letters' outlined with dry metal polish.

And it is not enough. He must try again and this time the 'true porch' emerges, 'square-cut, solid'. He opens his eyes and there indeed is the doorway into the hill. Then Malebron speaks and his words are crucial: 'The door will be open as long as you hold it in your memory.' In stories doors are so often magical. They are thresholds. No man's land; neither here nor there. Always we must try to open the door, cross the threshold, breach the barrier, and Miroslav Holub's poem 'The Door' provides the most compelling reasons for doing so, concluding with the unarguable:

> even if
>     nothing
>         is there,
> go and open the door.
>
> At least
> there'll be
> a draught.

When children write their own "threshold" poems, each poem must be a password. Their words must have all the power of the ancient 'Open Sesame'. Clifford Black's 'The Ford' on page 82 is such a poem. The words effect the crossing. So it is by dealing in the concrete images which make story and poetry, that children absorb and assimilate the abstractions of the creative process.

Most especially, the poems in this anthology were written by children learning to think, look, and listen within the good company of other writers. It is when children make that essential personal connection within a text that they recognise themselves and grow into the self-knowledge which is dependent on mastery of language. Poetry, as the most conscious and structured of all language, is the basis of the English teaching at Halesworth and the means by which children gain access to all the various genres. Poetry imposes an economy of form and structure within which they learn the power of the noun and verb and the need to discriminate carefully in order that adjectives and adverbs complement rather than compromise that power. They must weigh the merits of the strong active voice against the weaker passive and, above all, develop the listening ear which establishes criteria and, in the end, aspires to mastery. In this way, they learn to talk and think about language within a literary context which is by no means exclusive. Rather it encourages powers of criticism which discriminate between and adapt readily to other genres. The ability to discriminate, adapt and criticise is a natural by-product of developing thought, feeling, and sensibility. This is a rigorous route to literacy; it is also a sure one.

Particularly, it is when children have learned to make connections through leaps of imagination that they are best equipped for a technological age. These are the children who will write clear, correct reports, give and receive coherent instructions, and, most importantly, make their own unique contribution to an increasingly sophisticated society. The reductive face of sociolinguistics is today as effete and ennervating an alternative as the mindless rote learning of past decades. It makes concessions, compromises the imagination in trivial exercises in which lists are compiled, games played, charts plotted. There are, of course, areas of the curriculum where there are proper and meaningful contexts for all these activities. And English teachers have a special responsibility because it is through story and poetry that children will join the great and good company of writers within which they will receive our infinitely adaptable language. A literature-based syllabus which is structured and rigorous is, above all, catholic in application. This is its power.

The ideas behind the poems in this book are attempts to reconcile the reflective involvement of the poet in a moment of memory with the necessary detachment of the conscious artist. There must be an acute act of memory and, at the same time, a distancing, if children are to write well.

Ted Hughes's 'Thought-Fox' is a useful starting point for children growing into consciousness of their craft. Clearly, the poet writes about one particular fox. But a fox in a poem must aspire to universality in having about it something of all foxes everywhere. As Hughes says: 'It is a fox and a spirit. It is a real fox.' Moreover, as it nudges its way out of the poet's memory it is rather an amalgam of many foxes known. This is the power of the writer. As one of my own pupils said when questioned by his peers about an image in a 'fish' poem he had written: 'Well, actually, that was another fish.' Another day. Another pond. Another fish. This is not important because within the unifying power of his words, the poet connects the disparate, makes whole, transforms the particular into the universal. Hughes's *Poetry in the Making* read alongside the 'Thought-Fox' does more than initiate children into the poet's secrets or give them a glimpse into the rough note book of his mind, it explains the frustrations, the complexities of a task which can never ultimately succeed. When children like Marie on page 114 write their own 'Thought-Creature' poems, they attempt to name one particular creature by asserting its universality and in doing so they grasp, at least at an intuitive level, the processes of memory and imagination which must combine to make the poem.

Many of the poems in this book have been directly inspired by Ted Hughes's *What Is The Truth? A Farmyard Fable for the Young.* This is a dream sequence in which, tested by God Himself at the behest of the Son, the villagers aspire to describe their chosen creature in words so startling, so accurate, that they seem to challenge the very act of creation itself. They speak in their sleep because:

> '...In their sleep, they will say what they truly know...When they are awake, they are deepest asleep. When they are asleep, they are widest awake. Strange creatures!'

Sometimes they come tantalisingly close to the Truth, but, always constrained by their human condition, they must fail. God's dissatisfaction with their efforts is at once at odds with our own response to Hughes's earthy animal poetry and an endorsement of the sense of unattainable reality we glimpse in such writing. Again, this is the measure of the supreme dissatisfaction of the poet. However he chooses and patterns his words, the permutations are endless, limited only by our human condition.

Throughout the fable there is the special tension of knowing that, at the end, God Himself must answer His Son's question: 'What *is* the Truth?' His answer:

> 'The Truth is...that I was those Worms...And the Truth is...that I was that Fox. Just as I was that Foal...I am each of these things...'

is unsatisfying to the human ear because such ultimate Truth is beyond the grasp of our finite minds. We are permitted glimpses only, glimpses found in the daily round of our ordinary experience and caught in lines like:

18

> The Hare is a very fragile thing.
> The life in the Hare is a glassy goblet, and her yellow-fringed
> > frost-flake belly says: Fragile.
>
> The hare's bones are light glass. And the hare's face –
>
> Who lifted her face to the Lord?
> Her new-budded nostrils and lips,
> For the daintiest pencillings, the last eyelash touches.

Our preference for such animal poetry over God's stark 'I am...' is surely an affirmation of our human condition, rather than a rejection of the infinite. Moreover, at the end, as God returns to Heaven, the Son chooses to remain on Earth. And there is a doorway: 'And the middle of that cloud glowed like the gilded lintel of a doorway that had been rubbed bright.' Then the cock crows. This has such connotations within our culture that again we know our weakness, the vulnerability that flaws us, binds us to this earth where we must find our own Truth within ourselves if we are, at last, to turn outwards, articulate and whole.

Not only does *What Is The Truth?* enable children to write well, it equips them with the criteria they need to judge their own writing. They engage readily in the role-play which takes them on to the hillside prepared to speak the Truth of their chosen creature. They must enter a state of concentration which is dream-like in its intensity because they are being put under test by God Himself. Then there is the judging and they know that words, so elusive, so clumsy and wayward, cannot measure up to ultimate Truth. There is excitement in this knowledge because it is our destiny always to attempt the impossible.

Children cannot reflect upon or discuss their writing until equipped with the criteria which will make them their own severest critics. Fables like *What Is The Truth?* make such abstractions both concrete and accessible. Again, most especially, it is in the company of the poet and storyteller that children come into their rightful inheritance and receive the forms and symbols of the language within which they will know themselves, and the grammar within which they will make meaning. They must learn that while this grammar is not absolute, neither is it arbitrary.

Above all, English teachers never work alone. Poets and storytellers collude with them to entertain and instruct their pupils. The 'ghost' poems in this collection, for instance, were made possible by a reading of Leon Garfield's short story 'A Grave Misunderstanding'. Ghosts are dangerous. They are so bound by cliché they may dull the vision. Leon Garfield's story is set in a graveyard and has all the ingredients of the predictable. But this is a master story-teller who creates a ghost which is the very essence of the place, an elusive concentration of the earthy autumn air, leaf mould and pine. This is the basis of the children's poems – a ghost which is dynamic, with at least the latent power of a catalyst on her sur-roundings. Most importantly, her claim is on the senses. She is real. She *is* the place. The 'ghost' poems on pages 72-73 were written by children who had received a new perspective on the ordinary simply by reading a story which opened up areas of their own experience to new possibilities.

Other poems in this book arose out of a dream theme. Myth is a powerful impetus for writing and, in particular, I have found the Persephone myth a means of distancing children from this earth in order that they return to it with a sense of discovery and awareness. The very young child explores his world with a natural and keen curiosity. We see this in anthologies like Timothy Rogers's *Those First Affections*. Here there are tantalising glimpses of perception in words like three year old Patrick Buxton's:

> The owl is the mother of the dark.
> And the moon comes up
> From under the mud.

Spoken while being driven across Bodmin Moor, these lines testify to that response to place and atmosphere which is so much the peculiar vision of the young child. It is teachers' challenge to enable older children to recover this vision by looking as though for the first time ever in order to transform the mundane. The Persephone myth is one of those stories which must be told again and again. This is the acceptable face of rote learning – when familiarity deepens and illuminates perception and, in the end, resolves itself in understanding. Then the poem: Imagine you are Persephone trapped in the cold darkness of the underworld. Home-sick, you dream of the fruitful earth you have left behind. Again, within the dream sequence is the freedom to make unusual con-nections, sometimes even bizarre, but always apt.

This leads so easily to the making of myth for our own time: Imagine you are an astronaut exiled in the clinical austerity of your spacecraft. Your senses crave the good earth which is your home. This time the physical distancing returns the child to his familiar farms, fields, and gardens with a sense of discovery and urgency. Ursula LeGuin has said: 'The only way to the truly collective, to the image that is alive and meaningful in all of us, seems to be through the truly personal.' And strangely, we must lose our world in order to find it. In the 'astronaut' poems in this book, for instance, Sara savours the memory of crumpets because she has flown close to the moon whose pitted face restores reality and the time when there were crumpets for tea. Meanwhile Leanora's senses explore the minutiae of a lost world in lines like:

> He is yearning for his earth senses.
> He wants the smell of burning wood to swirl up
> And tickle his nose
> Like a coarse, rough feather from a bird on the earth.

The 'At Risk' section in this book represents the Halesworth children's close involvement with environmental issues. These are country children whose attitude to the natural world of the Waveney Valley is entirely unsentimental. Indeed, I hope their robust commonsense is an essential ingredient of their writing. But it is all too easy to take so much for granted and country children must learn to look in ways that regenerate thought and feeling.

Above all, as an English teacher, I do not teach environmental awareness. Rather, I attempt to inculcate it at the deepest level through poetry, fable, myth, and story. Nowadays there are so many attempts to identify and teach areas of moral and aesthetic concern outside the literary, scientific, or humane disciplines within which children should grow into sensibility and knowledge. Poetry, especially has the power to enable them to know their creation in the literary sense. This is to transcend easy sentimentality, reverse alienation and return them to the wilderness earth which has been their home for so many millions of years. From this homecoming grows an atavistic sense of recognition and a responsibility for an earth which must be held in trust by and for each succeeding generation.

Language and environment are inextricably linked and it is when children articulate a sense of kinship with earth that they acknowledge their source and affirm responsibility most surely. This is particularly evident in Matthew's poem on page 106 as he compares the death of Uncle George with the fall of a tree in the woods where the old man worked. Both come from Earth. Now they return to their beginnings:

> And his worn shoes
> Were the cut-off roots of the stricken tree
> Wedging him firmly
> To the living earth.

Sometimes there must be a sense of fearfulness. On pages 127-28, for instance, Stephen contemplates the the awesomeness of Nature in the crumbling cliffs of Dunwich as it sinks inexorably beneath the encroaching sea. Man's culpability in the changing climatic conditions which are accelerating erosion in this part of the Suffolk coast is, at least, a matter for conjecture and concern. Stephen's words restore to us a sense of our vulnerability, our place in the scheme of things. This is frightening but it is also the beginning of wisdom.

In poetry children find the detachment which confronts reality and refuses to compromise the facts. Therein lies the integrity which is the hallmark of both the poet and the scientist. But the poet must transform as well as instruct, so that as fact is assimilated, feeling is stirred and thought provoked. Then the beginning of wisdom becomes the beginning of hope for Planet Earth.

Above all, schools must value children's writing. Over the years the Halesworth children have attracted a wide readership which has fuelled the impulse to write for all levels of ability. I find that it is in the mixed-ability classroom that all children are most likely to fulfil their true potential. In this situation the less able are enabled through peer expectation (at least as important as teacher expect-ation) to read texts of a much deeper intellectual and emotional level than would otherwise be possible. There must be success and the criteria for success must be high and shared by teacher and children. For some children this will be no more than a line or an image read aloud and celebrated. Speaking has a deservedly high profile in classrooms today and discussion before, during, and after writing is an integral part of the process. But writing is a private act and when a poem is written there is a silence which must not be invaded. This is not to discount the value of collabor-ation but, in the end, it is when the child withdraws from the group in the private act of reflection that the poem is written. Then, the poem may be made public and the group may reconvene to listen, talk and criticise. This is a celebration of the poem which confirms the writer's sense of identity within his or her text. It is an integral part of the act of writing.

Some children go on to share their work with the local comm-unity in concerts and readings. Some have their work published and they know all the pleasure and status of authorship. This is most especially a shared experience, a matter for celebration with-in the whole school community. Also, and not least, children's writing should be widely accessible to the general public because it has much to offer.

In the brief pages of an Introduction it is possible to describe only a few of the ideas and strategies behind these poems. Much remains unexplored. Some children, for instance, have looked at paintings and poetry using the Tate Gallery anthology *With a Poet's Eye*. Others have entered the world of magic images in their 'Reflection' poems. For them George Tardios's words:

> The world is troubled
> With a lack of looking.
>
> ('Images. Cyprus 1961')

were a starting point. There is also that great parable of language and environment, Ursula LeGuin's *A Wizard of Earthsea* which has enabled generations of Halesworth children to reflect on the power, structure, and inexhaustible resources of language, and to write with new insight.

But the poems must speak for themselves, independently and outside the context of any vindication. It is enough to end with Ted Hughes's advice to teachers in his Introduction to *Poetry in the Making*: 'Their words should be not "How to Write" but "How to say what you really mean" – which is part of the search for self-knowledge and, perhaps, in one form or another, grace.'

JILL PIRRIE

*'just looking in a different direction'*
W. HART-SMITH

# 1. BEGINNINGS

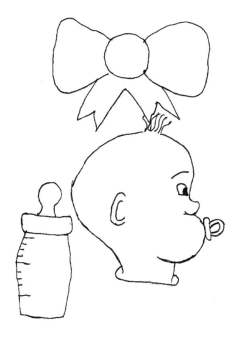

*Drawing:* ANNA BARTLETT, *12*

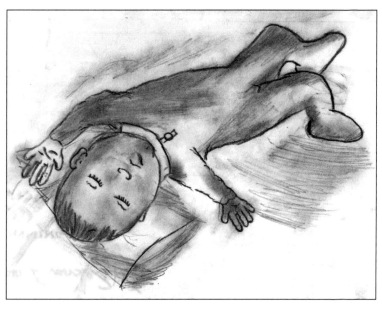

*Drawing:* **GRAHAM EVANS,** *11*

# Birth

Within the blood of the nettles
And the scorch of the sun
On a bed of plaited moss, you will find it.
Surrounded in dandelion sweat and apple sap
And a grassy green stain upon its spine,
It lies there, a bundle of bones in one heap.
The earth around it has the smell of coffee beans,
Freshly ground coffee beans.
In the background you can hear
The chorus of the cars climbing the hill
And the thud, thud, thud of the child's ball upon the ground.
Around the tiny cluster of veins and bones,
Are a thousand green needles
Threading the rain from tree to tree
And weaving cobwebs of willow silk.
The continuous drip of the clay rusty drain pipe
Is the lullaby for the baby rabbit.

EMMA BUCKINGHAM, *11*


# The Maternity Ward

Number 124,
Born 10,
Dead 2.
The maternity ward,
Dung hissing, the bloodstained floor, the piglets' inside skin.
The sow lies,
In her cot of metal bars,
Rolls of fat, tidal waves,
Underneath, no room for expansion.
A piglet stands in her tiny stiletto shoes,
Her heel stuck through the orange, plastic floor,
A sieve for muck and membrane.
Her mother gently woos her
With soft grunts of wisdom.

The piglet totters for her first found food
To find the wonder of outside and inside combined,
The pig's soft skin, gently woven by nature
Into a spider web fleece.
Her skin, the colour of heaven on a sunny day.
A new beginning
Ending for the day to come.
A whirl of blood.
No more.
And the piglet sucks on.

JOANNA TYLER, *13*


## First Sight

A flaming fire,
flames like people, star-shaped people dancing,
flickering red, orange, grey, and blue,
with crackling wood and snapping coal,
glowing red.

Bird egg green carpet
and chairs like mountains with snow on top.
Soft warm fur and black sandpaper pads...
and the first warming taste of milk,
of sweet milk on the tongue.

Then sleep...
crackling lullaby and dancing flames
with cradling fur;
ears envelop the puppy,
asleep in a twitching dream.

SAMANTHA SCRIVEN, *11*

# The Tadpole Is...

A priest,
Swimming among his congregation,
And wearing a rough robe of black
As he preaches to the shimmering stickleback.
The tadpole...
So soft, but so swift, and speedy, and slick.
The tadpole is an ink smudge
Spilt from the finest of pens.
It quavers like a shrill note,
Then stiffens to that one pose.
The tadpole is a stowaway.
Hiding.
Evacuating from its every home.
No safe place to hide for the tadpole.

MICHELLE BARNES, *12*


# The Red-Veined Dragonfly

The red-veined dragonfly is...
A pen
With the nib as a tail
Lying on four tiny rags of paper
Covered in little red lines
Shining brightly.
His two cartridge ball eyes
And pencil lead legs
Float through the air,
Gliding.
I watch him
Till he is out of sight,
Writing in the sky
That message...
He told me
How he had come from
A carcass

At the bottom
Of a deep, dank swamp.
And how he had
Fought his way
Through reeds and bulrushes
And met an army
Of water boatmen.
And had fought them,
Single-handed,
And been captured
And been put in a mud cage.
How he had broken out
And swum to the surface.
Then flown off at top speed.
And how the brightness
Nearly blinded him.
But he had fought it.
And now he is
A silver knight
Fighting for the light
In the world of
Air and clouds.

DAVID WHITEHAND, *11*

## Rachel

I gaze down.
Her large, midnight blue eyes stare back;
No tears when she cries.
Her arms wave about,
Fingers opening and closing like sea anemones
On the seashore,
With fingernail pearls on the end of each finger,
Shining in a cluster.
Hair sticking up,
But not untidy,
Just fuzzy,
Masses of it,

Completely covering her tiny head.
Her small rosebud mouth,
Blowing up an imaginary balloon,
Seems to smile,
Then laugh,
Almost shape up to whistle.
Her fascinating face is chubby,
Lively,
But peaceful.
Gown far too big,
Spindly arms and legs sticking out.
She doesn't cry.
My four hour old sister
Is contented,
Lying in my arms.
I hug her close,
My lovely sister.

PAUL SPARKES, *12*


## Nicholas

Nicholas is small to the onlooking world,
a frail miniature child,
but inside,
energy overflows
and his mind strengthens from day to day.

His small roundish face
is alight with a smile
which seems to be
four sizes too big for his mouth.
His ears,
almost pricked like a dog's,
waiting for the faintest noise.

His foot, bent, stiff
as if frozen,
ready to kick the ball.

31

His eyes stare
solidly, but almost delicately,
full with concentration,
aiming to hit the ball.

His foot swings
like a clock's pendulum.
The foot makes contact
and the ball bobs

for a short distance
like a car
using up the last drops of petrol...
Then it stops.

His face screws up
with disgust
like a shrivelled apple.
He turns
and starts running on his short stout legs,
almost like a partridge.

ROBERT ADCOCK, *11*


## First Day at Church

It was a day of relaxation,
supposed to be anyway.
Slowly we pushed open the door to the church.
Given a book, we took a seat.
I turned the fragile pages,
each page identical.
The smell was stale and the colour,
an aged yellow.
A scent of wallflowers floated on a breeze
and passed softly by.
Looking up, I found them,
standing in fresh water on the pulpit,
which took me back to my infancy
when the flowers were in full bloom

as I rolled on the fresh grass...
and the sun at its hottest.
A smell of candles filled the nave,
a touch of smoke and stale burning,
just like when dad over-cooked the toast.
The vicar trotted up the aisle,
a soft squeak in his shoes,
like a baby mouse.
He spoke in a deep crisp voice
as the sun lit the stained glass window
and a faint smell of old tobacco
drifted round and round in a loop of infinity.

STEPHEN MORRIS, *11*


## Creatures of the Classroom


By the table sits the lesser common schoolgirl,
clean, frosted,
with plaits carved from rock,
quite the opposite to the lesser common school boy,
in a corner, hiding from the hunter,
battered from fights to protect his territory.
His shorts hang loosely from bruised hips
and the markings are unique.
He lives in a wild environment,
never safe from the bellowing call
of the lesser spotted school teacher.
This species is distinguished by
a large Roman nose and jutting chin
and is usually found
in Victorian village primary schools in Suffolk;
though it has been sighted
around the coast of Scotland.
Then, the biggest of all creatures,
the check-pinnied dinner lady
who feeds the creatures of the classroom.

HANNAH EDWARDS, *13*

# First Love

School!...a strange place.
Love!...even stranger.
Kirstie Leeming...six years old,
yet a real shocker.
Pigtails like silky hemp
wrapped around two pieces of wire
held together by two red ribbons.
She would parade around the playground,
like a model on the catwalk.
Five year olds would stare.
Eight year olds would wolf whistle.
And teachers would sigh.
She wasn't at all boastful or proud,
but considerate and happy,
like a dizzy ballerina.
I adored her at primary.
I would sit staring at her, dreamily...
a drunken bat flying into the moon.
Until I was woken by my friend's elbow,
as the teacher passed.
Michael Aldridge stood in my way.
He was like the Berlin Wall;
I was West Germany;
and Kirstie was East Germany.
But those times are long gone
and the wall has come down.
Kirstie and I are older.
And just friends;
all is just memories
of primary days long gone.

BENJAMIN NORTHOVER, *13*

# 2. ENDINGS

*Drawing:* NATALIE WARD, *12*

# Chicken Lucky

I walk into the yard,
Mud squelching round my sodden boots.
The hen, a Sussex Black,
Struts, casting her foot into healthy mud.

The chicks tail behind.
Their tinsel-like down
Blows as a baby's ruffled hair.

I move suddenly, tugging at my boot;
The chicks scatter, all but one.
I step on a soft lump,
Like a sponge.
I lift my boot, and it reveals...

Dark red pipes and tubes
Moving as the chick lies,
Mouth wide, gasping for breath,
Eyes half closed,
Legs kicking widely into space.
Clawing for a hold.

Until...like a wound-down clock,
They stop,
The eyes closed.
Like an old man's,
They're grey and wrinkled.
I murmur a prayer
As other chicks use it
To clamber over,
The sticky grey tinsel
No longer fluffy.

I go for a shovel.

CAROLINE ENGLISH, *13*

# The Old Chicken

The old chicken cackled
Like an old woman,
Her beak strung open,
Gasping for air.
Her eyes,
Like deep holes in her head,
Sunken and dull.
She blinked, slowly, in the dim light.
Eyelids flicked down, and up again,
Thin flaps of skin,
Like scales of a snake.
Her crimson crest flopped over her left eye
Like a red beret.
The wattle, a double chin
Or a pink scarf,
Flapped as she turned her head.
Scaly legs,
Like the body of a worm,
Fold and wrinkle, loose flaps of skin.
Tail feathers overlapping one another
As a fan of cards.

The old chicken gargled softly
As if trying to sing herself to sleep.
Then pecked slowly in a puddle in front of her.
The barn was dark,
But a patch of light lit up the two hen boxes in which she lay.

Her neck hung out of the box
Like a dog's tongue from its mouth
And dangled limply in the puddle.
Her eyes closed, as if still sleeping.
She gargled no more.

SALLY CLIFTON, *12*

37

# Winter

A gull, its wings stiffly flapping,
Calls to a mate who'll never see home.
The landscape looks as if
Feathers by the million have fallen off a bird.
And a dead tree flowers again.
Flowers that no one can pick.

A goose, scrabbling frantically,
Falls through to abrupt silence.
And a sparrowhawk, so frail,
But made deadly with hunger,
Flicks along the hedgerow.

And last year's nettles,
Stork's legs in a sea of white,
Killed by the frost,
While a swallow lies,
Dead and entombed in ice,
The perfect grave.

MATTHEW LINE, *11*


# Mastitis

How she suffers,
A cow.

When her udder is hard,
As cold as winter's web,

She strikes her calf away,
As it tries to suck,
Strikes, not meaning to hurt!

She bellows!

The icicles form on her breath.

38

Her udder bursts,
Rotted,
White milk flows,

Rapids on water.

She falls,
Sleeping death.
The ice overtakes her,
And the cold wind tears her away.

MARNIE SMITH, *12*

# Death of a Mole

A furry drawstring purse
Wobbles through the field.
Blind in the upper world
But a ruler downstairs.
Its body black
But its nose brown from furrowing,
All its tunnels dug out gently,
Not ploughed like a bulldozer.
The calm pace of its scuffing
Makes it a genteel ruler.
The mole is not a savage,
But dinner coils past,
The purse opens
And dinner rolls into the inner lining.
Hunger satisfied,
The mole scurries on up to our world,
Blind again.
The farmer has his shovel;
The guillotine descends.

MATTHEW SHEPHERD, *12*

# Mole Trapping with Grandad

The heavy thump of hobnail boots
And the sharp retort
As a moling stick strikes a flint.
You can feel the soft lack of earth
As you push a stick
With a quick jerk into a tunnel...

Then, the grind of the jaws
As they slowly open and click into place.
Tiny droplets of dew
Slide off the grass
As the turf is lifted
And the trap is slowly pushed in.
And you catch a whiff
Of stale air as it forces its way out.

Then sitting, after setting a good number of traps,
Under my favourite oak,
Eating a packed lunch,
And leaning back to look at nests
As they sway and rock in the wind...
I wonder if they get seasick.

Then, it's back off to the well-remembered spot
To dig up the trap, to see a dead mole,
A cold forgotten pair of ear muffs,
Lying limp in my hands.
I suddenly push it into the bag.
I shrug and tell myself,
Never again.

MATTHEW LINE, *11*

# Grandad

Grandad smelled of fish boiled in milk
And liquorice root on which he continuously chewed,
Grumbling about taking pills,
Although they were all that kept him alive.

There was a pile of pipe cleaners
By the fireplace
Smelling of dust
And used too many times,
Like the bleached chicken bones
On the birdtable.

He had been working on his allotment
In his better trousers
So they got muddy
And he had scrubbed them
With a wire brush.
Then had to try and darn them again.

The hardened globule of denture cream
Looked like a birdsplash
On the side of the vase,
In which flowers melted into the water,
Staining the glass at the waterline.

When I was very small
There was always a toy phone
On which we played a game
In which he ordered sacks of potatoes.
So I used to bring them round,
Out of the garage.
He gave me 5 pence per sack.

Then he died,
Mixing with smells
Of camomile tea
And boiled fish.

EDWARD LINE, *13*

# Grandad

I watch Grandad pick up a potato.
With his other hand
He rubs the wet mud off with his thumb.
His eyes scan the potato,
Searching for blight or slugs.
His crinkled hand slowly puts down
The potato.
A drop forms on the tip of his nose.
He shakes his head.
The drop falls to the ground
And soaks into a clod of mud.
He groans with pain as he stoops.
He coughs and it sounds as if a small baby
Is choking in a cave.
His hair waves up and down as
He moves.
He finds a sack
And carefully starts to put them in.
The sack rustles as the potatoes roll in
And make a thud as they hit the others.
Then all is quiet as the bag is full
And all I can smell
Is fresh earth and the flavour
Of tobacco on Grandad's jacket.

MARK CLARKE, *12*


# Gran

Gran sits at the old scrubbed pine table,
riddled with woodworm.
'Only worth a halfcrown in old money,' she says.
She breakfasts on homemade soda bread and marmalade.
In the wink of an eye the breakfast is gone
and then she's on to her second helping.
She must be ravenous, I think to myself,

as I watch her old hands, with veins thick as knitting needles,
spread each slice of bread with butter.
She stretches and burps with satisfaction.
Then she slowly clears the table,
and even more slowly she washes the dishes.

She takes down ingredients from a shelf in the larder,
bought in bulk because its cheaper...
flour, salt and baking soda which she mixes together
with milk and some water.
She kneads the dough over and over,
her old wrists rising and falling as if by instinct.
Then she stokes the old oven and leaves it to heat through.
At last she puts the baking tray into the oven
and within minutes an invisible perfume wafts through the kitchen.
Out comes the bread, crisp and light brown,
with a cross on the top.
Gran, exhausted, drops into a cane chair and watches television.
Her old face, crinkled with worry lines
and tanned by years of working in the open,
creases into a huge contented smile,
like the flat round shape of a soda bread loaf.

EUGENE COLLINS, *11*


## Tiny Tovell


He mumbles about a wife
he almost had
until a shell killed her.
Now he wanders,
his coat torn to shreds beyond repair,
lasting probably since the war.
His shoes, bright and shiny,
probably used to a bit of spit and polish.
His arms point, angled away from his body,
as he looks right through you
to see the other side,
cutting himself off,

shocked into oblivion,
not knowing who you are or where you are,
staring at an object and going for it.
Some say he's mad.
Some say he's extraordinary.
But the only thing wrong with Tiny Tovell is that he's
Shellshocked.
Not mad or extraordinary, like everyone says.
But in a mind of his own.
Mumbling and grunting,
walking along the road.

MARK HARDACRE, *13*


## The Drowning

On the river opposite –
A man in a canoe.
Down the rapids he went
Faster than an arrow.
He knuckled against a rock.
He capsized.
He slammed his head on the bottom
And stayed there.
Unconscious.
I sat, hoping he would surface.
Quickly,
The lifeguard slicked into the river.
Later...
The man lay there,
A dead salmon.
His friend cried.
And I who didn't know this man
Cried...
A little.

DARREN FELLER, *12*

# **3.** REFLECTIONS

*Drawing:* ELIZABETH WILCOCK, *12*

*Drawing:* ADAM FERJANI, *12*

# Reflection

I sat and stared
At a world I knew,
But didn't.
The reflection rippled
On the oily surface
Of the vase.
The light was pink,
My face dark.
The table hung
Like a hammock,
And the walls
Domed in around me.
The fruit bowl was swollen.
Over the side of the vase
Drooped wilting flowers
With petals like waxed pencil sharpenings.
And as I reached to touch one,
My hand, green, grew
And fingers stretched and widened.
My little finger
As big as the rest,
And my hand looked unbalanced.
I held the room;
From one end of the table to the other
Loomed my fingers.
As I let go they shrank
And I just sat and stared
At a world I knew.

THEA SMILEY, *13*


# Sailing With Reflections

The jib-sheet
Slaps at weeds,
But penetrates them

As if they were just images in a hologram.
My face,
Cushioned on a cloud,
Ripples,
Like a silken scarf
Trailed over sand
Left furrowed by the ebbing tide.
A seagull dives,
Meeting his twin at the water line,
While a Happy Shopper Coke can
Drifts through the sleeve
Of my life-jacket,
And out through the neck,
Bobbing up and down over my chest.
My hair,
Tangled with weed,
Blows haywire in the water.
Stones, debris, murk
Show through my transparent body
As we glide over the estuary.
A pine tree on the far bank
Stretches up to the sky
And down to the deeps
Like the North and South
Points on a compass.

A duck
Swims synchronised
With her double.
Never pausing to wonder
At this topsy-turvy world of
Reflection.

I trail my fingers
Loosely in the water.
The reflection fans out,
Splintering,
Like tresses of hair blown back in a wind.
Never to be captured
Quite that way
Again…

LARA MAIR, *12*

# Rockpool Reflection

Morning came.
Red rays threw the water picture.
The pinky sun hung from the weed on the bottom,
Its heat too great and harsh.
Cold water fought back,
And the heat sizzled out on the surface.
Where a faint rainbow
Filtered on the back of the crab
Whose claws clutched the light grey clouds.
The gulls floated,
Breaking the surface,
But without a quiver.
On the stones lay little barnacles.
From the sky's many-a-face.
The salty breeze backcombed my hair.
And the surface rippled.
I looked up and the clouds smiled
And melted away.
Just like the image in the rockpool.

JESSICA BROWN, *12*


# The Shimmering Book

A pond,
A pad with many pages,
A pen made of light.
A new face shimmering on a new page.

Tiny insects
Scamper around.
Secretaries laden with work.
The face still shaking,
Shaking with silence.
The same face on every clean page.

A book shimmering with pictures.
The insects
Run around,
Busy drawing a face,
With bubbles.
Carved with detail,
On a page,
In a book,
On a pond.

SCOTT SPINDLER, *12*


## Reflections

Ripples on a pond
Delicate and mild,
Yet ferocious,
Dividing your head
In a bloodless way.
The water settles,
Like tracing paper
The surface traces the sky;
It films the moving,
It reads you like a book,
Uncannily,
Upside down, and backwards.
This time the dog does not jump for the bone
Yet tries to stroke the underwater cats
Who dart, like their cousins,
For a safe haven.

The pond is liquid quartz.
A two-way mirror
For the water beetle.
A transparent cover
Better than steel
For it can never be dented
By the swift blow.
A water beetle

Does not know what he is,
For the water can cause him no
Reflection
Which he can like or loathe
To have inflicted
Upon himself
Night or day
To haunt him,
Taunt him;
Or is his mind too small
To worry?

CLIFFORD BLACK, *13*


## Reflections

The rushes on the banks of the lake
Stretch out to touch.
The reflection of the old mansion
Is so still…
A painting,
A perfect mirror image.

A pond skater on a lily
Pulls on his boots,
Laces tight.
Off he goes.
He spins around and around,
Dancing on his reflection,
Stretching it.

A frog jumps.
The water pot spills,
The painting runs.

GEMMA WHITE, *12*

# Time

My Grandma lived in a basement flat.
I imagined it as an underground hole,
And my Grandma, a creature, hiding scared
From the outside world.
Caught in time.
The staircase bent around
Like a huge Chinese Dragon
With a million bright colours
In the carpet.
The carpet itself was shaggy and heavy...
A big, hairy dog could easily get lost in it,
Or so I thought.
From the window two rectangles of light
Melted onto the carpet.
The dust flew,
Caught in those two rays of light,
Caught like Grandma,
Caught in time.
And if I, too, stepped into those rectangles,
Would I be caught forever, like dust?
Would I be caught like Grandma?
For the very last time.

JOANNE IRELAND, *13*


# The Time of Day

A tiny, near-bald rat,
Out of a sun-coloured mother.
He grew, suckling milk as warm and rich
As compost.
A knock-kneed puppy,
One ear tumbled over his eye,
Like a stubborn forelock.
His fur was imitation gold velvet,
The gold at the fringe

Of a fresh sun-risen autumn stream.
It is morning.

He has grown,
His legs have straightened,
His coat has mellowed,
His muscles ripple as water-filled balloons,
As he leaps, the blue and green ball
Caught.
In memory
As he comes to earth
The sun has climbed; it is noon.

He will tire,
The balloons will burst
And the water drain away.
The blue and green ball
Will wear thin, and rot from damp.

The light from his sun-coloured mother
Will have been extinguished long ago.
He will lie in front of a new fire,
Lapping cold treated milk,
As hollow to taste
As licking Christmas envelopes for the world.
And his coat will lose its shine,
Grow unfocused,
The halo of a summer sunset
In the late evening.

And his face will wrinkle,
His sight will blur,
Eyes trying to look through seawater.
The new-born kitten,
Trying vainly to pump blood through his ancient body
Will give up, tired of work,
And he will die.
For the Sun-dog's coat will shine no more;
For one day all stars will die,
And there will be eternal light.

STEPHEN GARDAM, *13*

# Fossil

Small detail sustained in time, right down to a fish's scales,
printed shadow and light.
A shell protecting its treasure,
never to be broken.
A stone skeleton.
A snail a thousand ages old,
bailed out into the cold rock...
Hard prints of a once lived life,
light filtering the mind's eye
until the world's shape is moulded into stone.
Corrugated iron, rock, cobweb?
Ridged-ribbed-rock.
Grooves engraved into mud, into rock, into our minds.
Or a wax moulded chrysalis, waved, wax burnt to a crisp.
I touch it. It is taut,
pulled into naked design
and left to be folded and kneaded into shape
in the soft rock –
made into hard rock.
God's art work is in the form of a fossil.

JESSICA BROWN, *12*


# The Goldfish

The goldfish is
A gold bracelet
Dropped in the sea
By a pirate
In the days of old
And magically transformed
Into a fish.
Then it swam
Into a treasure cave,
Half underwater,
And was rightfully named

The goldfish.
One day
An underwater diver came,
So fascinated by the goldfish's shine
That he put him
Into his glass helmet
And took him to the surface.
And ever since
He has been kept
In the diver's glass helmet
On the sideboard,
Swimming round and round
Like a tiny boat in a whirlpool.

DAVID WHITEHAND, *12*


## 'Shelter Scene: Bunks and Sleepers'
*(from the pen, chalk, watercolour and gouache
of the same name by Henry Moore)*


They lie, frightened,
cocooned in their own shelter.
They try desperately to stop the noise,
hiding their heads with their arms,
six kittens pawing their faces.

No one sleeps in this shelter tonight.
They are restless, like nervous children.
Worried about relatives,
dead relatives.
Though these families don't know that.

Outside they hear a fire bell,
carried through London
on the howling wind.
The dust scratches at the door.
It tries to shelter too.

The lantern hangs,
creating a dull light.
Its swaying and creaking
reminds them of the pub sign where they live.
'The Romping Donkey',
hardly a name to be taken seriously.
And now it's gone,
caught in last night's raid,
but living in their memories.

Suddenly the lantern burns out.
Then, a gigantic bang,
an explosion upon all explosions hits them,
like a giant puff ball,
thrown by a playing child.

Lives burn out...
Like the lanterns...
And the all-clear sounds.

WILLIAM MAIR, *12*


## 'Ennui'

*(From the painting of the same name*
*by Walter Richard Sickert)*


A case of stuffed birds imprisoned by glass,
Flecks of colours that the artist has captured.
An old woman stands in the corner of her kitchen.
Gazing at them,
She is also trapped,
But by the finest of brushes and the thinnest of paint.
Her husband,
Slumped in an old wicker chair,
Stains the air with his cigar.
Remembering...when he was young,
And the birds he trapped.

He wants them all to be free.

GEMMA WHITE, *12*

# 4. FARM, FiELD AND GARDEN

## (AND AN AMERICAN CAT IN LONDON)

*Drawing:* GEORGINA HUCKER, *13*

# Farmyard Chatter

There they are, every day without fail.
Leather breath and graciously plodding,
The local gossips.
Listen to them whisper, listen as they trip
Over the caked ground.
Fresh straw...smelling like that
Box of Weetabix I opened last week.
Sizzling silage in large grey tanks.
Hear it bubble, then splurt against the cold tin.
Breathe in,
And your lungs will fill with roasting dung
And fresh cut grass.
I passed through that farm;
The smells pierced the back of my throat.
And those graciously plodding local gossips
Whispered and stared.

EMMA BUCKINGHAM, *12*

# The Cow

Warm desperate eyes
Looking down on me
Pitifully, as if it was terrible to be human.
Ears folded like wrinkled-up shavings;
Softly smiling mouth with strings of spit
Hanging from the gentle pinkness of lips.
Warm smelly breath reaches out to
The cold air like the steam from boiling milk.
Wet nose like a sponge
With drips of mucus running down it,
Then mixing with the strings of spit.
The udder is baggy with milk,
Drooping down towards the cobbled ground.
Shoulders sticking out
With skin pulled tightly around them.

And the tail – muddy and soaked in rain
Swishes carefully from side to side.
The cobbled yard is embedded in
A layer of mixed-up cowpat,
Steam rising thickly from it.
The cow, a beautiful caring creature;
And we take her milk,
And sometimes her calf and her life.

KIRSTY BUTCHER, *11*


## The Silent Cowshed

Lumpy mud settles down,
With snow over it like sugar lumps.
The cows,
Black and white minstrels
Lying under a roof.
The hay,
Frosted.
An aeroplane flies over the cowshed,
Sounding like a cat purring.
I shout to the cows,
'Come along here, you lazy cows,
Food's ready.'
My voice falls dead and small
Into a silence,
Like a stone slipping into a pond,
Without a splash.
Sealed up in a silence you can almost touch.

DENISE REVELL, *12*

# Truth of the Cockerel

Bold, upright, head held high with pride,
Haughty, a prince going into battle,
To defend and protect his ladies,
Scales like fish skin on his legs,
Spurs like ivory tusks.
A gentleman with gold sequins on a shirt of silk,
But ready for rugby in padded football shorts.
He shrieks like a horn, telling everyone to take action,
And charges the foe.
He returns defeated,
Whimpering,
Deserted,
Alone,
And sits on his perch in the twilight.

RHYS HARPER, *12*


# Conker

Apple blossom blows,
gently
down onto the hutch.
A guinea watches from the wire;
it can't be snow!

He waits at the wire;
bored, he nibbles at a wisp of hay.
His deep dark eyes scan about,
looking for predators.
He stops nibbling.
A noise.
He heard something.
He turns and runs into the undergrowth,
and camouflages himself.
An army recruit in battle.

The scuffle has ruffled his hair.
He has rosettes on his back;
it is as if someone
has blown on his hair,
hair which is soft to touch,
yet looks coarse,
like the Timothy grass that grows by the back door.

And while I feed him,
Chestnut peeps out from under the hay
as the blossom blows.

SARA WORTS, *12*


## The Pheasant


The pheasant is the convict of the bracken world,
as he runs stumbling haphazardly.
A line of beaters stands ready to advance.
The signal is given
and the air rings
to men's bellowing voices
and sticks banging the bracken
that cracks under the frying sun!
The convict is sighted
and the only way is up,
up into the vast empty palette they call the sky.
He takes off like an uncoordinated puppet,
but where is the getaway car?
As the pheasant heads over the trees,
The enemy works the puppet.
He looks down the silver-plated kaleidoscope eyes
at the double barrel gun
and in a feather ruffling
screaming
eyes rolling second,
the pheasant falls like a clod of soil
earthed by a shot that drained the Electricity of life.

A last nerve flickers
and he dies.
Now he hangs by his neck in our garage.

HANNAH EDWARDS, *12*


## The Peacock

A Japanese fan,
Each feather an old man's eye.
A circular disc of fishy scales,
Splinters of blue glass tinted by the sun,
Oriental colours held in a china vase.
The peacock is the petals fallen from many a flower,
Stuck with morning dew and stitched with spider's web.

This peacock is a Prince riding his white horse,
And wearing a cloak of rainbow.
He swoops away to the maiden's rescue...
Then, he is the turquoise sun,
The fire in the sky,
The shimmering haze on a tarmacked road...
The Prince arrives and the fanfare plays.
He releases his legs like a vulture to his prey.
Grabbing the ground with onion-ring feet.
And, slowly, he stops and stands tall.
He combs his feathers with fork-like claws.
He stalks on.
A proud and particular creature,
Made into a word.
Beauty in disguise.

MICHELLE BARNES, *12*

# Cat

I saw it...
Suspended in a dull spectrum of
Straight edges curved
And muzzy sharpness.
Black from Shadow and Birth,
Light and Earth.
Caught with its hand in the till.
Found out.
A simpleton,
In a deep velvet gown,
Soft and cuddly...
No.
A hardened criminal,
Wearing a balaclava and jumpsuit.
Wads of ill-gotten notes
Lie bulging out everywhere
On its burnt wood body,
Cracked into a thousand tiny snippets of wire.
Its puffed out sleeves are
Crowbars, heavy with power,
Light with arrogance.
Bulging long at one end,
Short at the other,
Studded with diamonds of lead.
Its face held me,
As it held itself,
Clear, yet shrouded,

Showing itself naked
As a poor creature caught
In some harmless mischief.
But hiding the charlatan.
A black angel,
Hell-bent on hell.
Whiskers and nose,
Probing out a victim.
Eyes,
Gold watches streaked by fire,
Glazed, corrupted,

Yet totally in command.
Almost.
Ears,
Fat feathers pruned to perfection
Arranged tastefully in black fur.
Twin cloth caps
Rakishly placed
For its old fashioned interests.
And its tail,
Young and vibrant,
Boasting to do anything.
But the reality is nothing.
Its teeth,
White splinters from a cracked china marble.
The implements in ten hundred deadly games.

Scene: Anywhere.
Suspect: The Cat.
Accused.
Gone.

STEPHEN GARDAM, *13*


## American Cat in London


Dressed smartly in his fur coat,
The cat is a businessman,
With no guarantee.
The Cat,
With his gas mask face,
Is a dirty dealer.
Cat Capone is back in town.
The Cat,
Carried away with his shortcomings,
Arrested,
Charged,
Imprisoned.
Bail paid and Cat walks free.
Cat's eyes stab the dark,
As he strides out of his house,

His coat almost merged into the Victorian bricks of the terrace.
His whiskers, a moustache,
His claws
Are his pens,
And his mouth, his briefcase
This Cat's ears are Sky television receivers.
As used by his nextdoor neighbour.
The Cat is a cat burglar no more.
Yes, the Cat is a businessman,
In a big bad backyard.

JAMES NOBLE, *12*


## Winter Churchyard

Not a churchyard,
A courtyard
Armed with white wigged gravestones.
Silent with silence.
Their dirt grained faces
Stare with stiff necks
At one another,
Each one,
Guarded by its own bumped-up shadow.

The church's eye slit windows.
Lost,
Lost in the winter's white.
Its frost-frilled doorway
Peppered with boot grit,
Swimming in footprint puddles;
Escaping water hangs from the gutter
Caught in the cold,
Waiting for its freedom.
The sun pokes its head out
From the smoke-patched sky.
Unlocking the trees from their winter sentence.
For how long?

OLIVER MACDONALD, *13*

# The Graveyard

Dull colours,
Sorrow and sympathy,
A boy in a picture,
An unborn baby,
New-bedded soil
On unsettled turf.
A sad tune
With a meaning so true,
A sweet verse,
A white cloth,
A last footstep,
An old vicar,
A plaque on the wall,
A silver cup,
An everlasting candle,
And the carvings of the woodlouse
That, as skilfully as a craftsman's,
Are embedded
In the wood for evermore.

SIMON HONEYWOOD, *11*


# Summer

Summer smells like...
Pot pourri and the bunches of daisies
Peeping out of the rich grass,
Green with goodness.
It fills your lungs and makes you gasp.
And the dog puts his nose into the breeze
And closes his eyes.
The warm smell of rabbits alerts him.
He races, transformed into a greyhound.
You can't stop him now.
I run after him.
He stops, puts his nose into the silent breeze...

Suddenly, a burst of energy
And he leaps into action!
I can't see him anywhere.
Suddenly two ears pop out of the field,
Where wild flowers grow.
He is running, barking,
Sniffing the fragrance that flows out of them.

JUSTIN BLOOMFIELD, *12*


## Flaming June

The pond skaters
Skate on a tightened elastic band
Stretched too far.
It breaks with a snap and a plop
As a gold fish moves.
Ringlets flow out,
Like the ripples in a wavy hairstyle.
The cress weed with coal roots
Grows through the wire bird-stopper.
My tadpoles, like two developed apostrophes,
Live in amongst that cress,
Legs of it making a slalom course
Upon a sloping ledge.
A frog sits sunbathing
On the waterlogged branches
Of a fallen tree
And the fiery sun
Suntans the field
Towards its future harvest.

EMMA GRAVES, *13*

## Apple Fire

Tall grass
Stood sharp
And smoke boiled up,
As we sat in the damp steam
Of the roasting apples.
Apples, once sour, once tough,
Now smelled bruised, over-ripe.
Flames stood like warriors,
With water as their only conqueror.
Not afraid, they stabbed, carelessly,
Through the fretting fruit.
The skins sagged, red,
Bloodstained,
Rapidly browning.
Loose, like the cotton and cloth round a button hole.
A button hole letting a button gradually out of its grasp...
Tall grass
Stood sharp,
While we let smoke bellow up in our faces
And pulled the grass away from the pampas
To keep it alive...
Poisonous fumes made our eyes water.
Whipping, coarse smoke exploded in our throats.
Our clothes stank
And the apple waistcoats fell,
Green to black,
To reveal the flesh,
Smooth,
Soft,
A pleasant warmth to swallow.

JEFFREY BIRD, *13*

# Snapdragon

A frilled lip of gold, of gold dust falling from sunshine,
The puckered mouth of the silently angry dragon,
Wavering up on his green stalk tail,
Waiting.
Curl of scarlet velvet, his fire scorching the dust,
Licking the wall in a cluster of flames.
In cockerel comb splendour, the plump cushion
Is heavy. And the delicate neck is wrapped in wax paper
For protection.
A splash of rippling flag and he is crowned with gold fringing,
Triumphant but brooding.
He is a cavalier's doffed hat, flamboyant feather
Picked out in gold.
Battle colours charge the wind on a beige charger of lace,
His jousting pole, a beam of piercing sunlight,
Pretending to be jolly.
But the flushed skirt of rage does not fool anyone...
The tight collar strangling the light,
And the false smile, weatherbeaten into his lips.
The stem is strong green raffia,
But elastic, stretching further than it should,
So that when you pinch, he lurches to bite,
Clamping sour lips on flesh.
But the crusty dragon, old and lemon lipped
Cannot harm.
He has little perfume.
That which he has is stolen from the rose and dried.
In winter, he shrinks back
With rheumatism, his one master, the wind.
But always back in the summer.
A bumble bee, sensing blossoming danger,
Buzzes near and far.
The hum mingles with the hiss
Of wind on earth and leaves.
The hiss of the dragon.

EMMA WALKEY, *13*

## Pitcher of Nepenthes

It hangs,
Its beer mug pitcher brimming over
With the fine ale of its digestive juices.
Its latest meal,
A Queen Bee,
Fresh from the nest,
Its wings stuck to its sides
By the treacle-like substance.
Its leaves are spread out like flames
And the red and yellow mix
To create a miniature sun,
Drawn down to earth
By a fragile green thread.
Its rim,
Like a lover's lips,
Leads down to a witch's cauldron,
Brewing and bubbling with the remnants of a fly,
Drawn into this rank pit.

KEVIN LAWLESS, *13*

# 5. DREAMS AND HAUNTINGS

*Illustration:* DANIEL HALL, *12*

# Ghost of the Sea

Ancient fingers
Search for you
Through to your soul,
Shiver down your spine as if her hand is on your back.
Her fingernails of fish scales...
And she is biting your mind.
Mist is reaching to your heart
When it crawls over the frantic waves.
The waves foam,
The strands of her past life.
The cliffs crumble like her chalk teeth
Where seaweed hangs.
Little shells, carrying the water,
Climb to the beach
Like maidens of old time
Fetching water from the well.
Whistle in the wind and the ghost will appear.
Her face,
Lacy like fishing tackle,
Moulded from a gull's nest...
Feathers and cracked shell left behind in her dreamless mind.
Her silk cloak and cobwebs hang from her armpits;
Her bleached hair
And her wispy voice tell you...
'Never come again.'

ROBERT FILBY, *12*


# The Ghost of the Orchard

She walks through overgrown grass,
With apple silk feet.
Her face is round and sweet as an apple,
Yet tainted with the sourness
Of apples gone bad, dreams gone bad.
Crystallised thoughts, held still in an empty head,

With beads that rattle as she walks, talks.
Her breath is the mist on cold morning air,
As her dry silk ball gown, moth eaten, brushes past
Dead trees and wilting flowers.
She smells of old cider and mothballs
And apples in wicker baskets,
Tunnelled by wasps.
Her eyes are twirling apple pips.
Sad and forgotten.
She shakes her head and her coils of ebony hair,
Like blackberries, shake too,
Shaking out smells of smoky straw and rotten fruit.
Her voice is like a feather falling through the air...
'Who will dance with me?'

The wind shall dance with you, my dear,
Dance a cider waltz around your trees,
Through your veins and your hollow voice
The wind blows through and through...

'Who will dance...?'

EMMA WALKEY, *12*


## Moon Thoughts


White
Against the dusky dome of sky,
Painted with stars that spin white light wetly.
Old,
Marked black from soot and ashes
From its own long ago funeral,
Its sunken in face imprinted
On its crusty dry surface.
Channels thrashed in by once flowing rivers,
Icy and bubbling like a frosted breeze,
Choking with weed and bright eyed fishes,
Roots and trees bursting from the ground,
Like green silk thread pushing through cloth

On a flashing needle.
People laughing, buying round, bright fruit
From market stalls with stout ladies,
Mountains sprayed with snow like shaving foam
Peeking, piercing the dark blue sky,
Like swords buried in the ground.
Then...
The river's icy channel, filled with emptiness,
Only fishes' bones imprinted on dry rock.
Rock on rock, rock on rock.
The mountain's pinnacle is grey and dry.
The lake's hole is dry and splashed with dark.
The people are gone, the bones melting into
The vast whiteness, crumbled with charcoal.
There is no form of life,
But many forms of death.
Shadowed by darkness around it,
It spins on, its surface rolled with black ink.
The face on its face does not smile.

EMMA WALKEY, *12*


## Memories from Space


I miss the Earth from up here.
Now I see it as a roller
Used for printing patches on newly born cows.
I remember walking through the fields
In which they grazed...
The smell of dung, earth, dead leaves and twigs
Was a smell sweeter than honey.
Now missed but before unnoticed.
The leaves, fossilised trees,
And me fossilised within my
        Memories.

MARIE FENN, *13*

## Astronaut

He stood, gazing at the earth, dreaming of his flower garden...

Green tips of seedlings poking from the compost,
opening their leaves to be warmed by the sun,
the sun bouncing off the greenhouse:
tomatoes turned orange to red
and worms crawled in the damp soil, sunning their skins.
His wife planted seedlings; making a hole with her index finger,
she eased in the marigold.

He missed catching the 7.56 to Leeds,
the click of the typewriter printing A's and E's
on the headed note paper.
He missed the tone of the telephone
and the lift saying 'Going up'.
Then there were...

Sunny afternoons on the heath
wandering down sheep paths,
in amongst the heather.
Heather, a blaze of colour like fire,
reds and oranges.
And when he got home there would be
crumpets rich with butter,
crumpets like the moon...

Like the moon.

SARA WORTS, *12*

## The Earthsick Astronaut

He is yearning for his earth senses.
He wants the smell of burning wood to swirl up
And tickle his nose
Like a coarse, rough feather from a bird on the earth;

He wants the sight of a fire,
The flickering fish tails
That make his eyes see nothing else;
He wants to taste bacon, the real bacon,
Tingling on his tongue to evoke
The smell, the sound, the flavour...
He wants the touch of cold air on his skin;
Air, a free spirit, teasing, running;
A brush-past kiss on a warm cheek is
His memory;
And then...the sad things;
Gravestones like babies' teeth, yet
Decayed with lichen and moss.
But still he is yearning,
Yearning for air, for fire,
For Earth.

LEANORA DACK, *12*


## A Ploughing Dream


At midnight – still.
The old plough turfed up clumps of wet mud.
A slash with a whip
and a kick up the ass.
'Goa on!'
roared the farmer.
A great crack in the purple sky
opened daylight for a split second.
Gran's old tablecloth
flapped in the gale as rain started to pour –
she'd left it out all night.
The leather strap unreeled
to slash its guts
to bloody ribbons, slithering to a bucket of eels.
The horse pulled away –
snapped the straps,
heeled on its hind legs
and stumped the cart with its front teeth –

the size of building bricks.
Storming off into darkness,
only two massive haunches showing,
like loose muscles dancing.

The farmer
stumbled to the ground
and started to pull –
heaving –
slipping his feet
in the mud,
The thunder roared
and the sky reopened,
leaving a maroon mist.
His muscles snapping
and breaking all over,
getting nowhere.
The plough no longer ploughing,
he fell to the mud,
studding his back –
slapping his arms down to the puddles,
tying his wrists down with his whip.
He gave up,
naked.

ROBERT FILBY, *12*


## Dream of the Fisherman


The line sways in the breeze.
On the end,
A bright orange float.
There is a tug.
A tug of strength,
As if gravitation pulls on the sea.
Then,
In a flash of light,
Silver leaps from the lake,
And lands on the bank,

Where flames form a circle.
This fish is a demon.
The sea demon.
It darts,
And with a flip of its fins
It is a bird,
Beak shimmering like petrol in a puddle.
Each scale is a feather,
A raindrop on a window.
It swoops
Back into the sea.
Its world forever.
I wake
To find mist merging over the lake,
And I leave,
With an empty net,
But a full mind.

SUZANNE ALDERTON, *12*


## Hibernating Dreams


I must sleep...
I don't know why...
I sink down down down
To dream of leaves of fire
And apples rotting.
I smell the musty smell
Of wet leaves.
The trees shedding their last few flames of life
Before sleeping...

The misty evenings of warm autumn days,
A sensation of mouth-watering
Bugs and beetles.
The leaves that fall
Are falling to death,
Falling from a forgotten tree.

Everything is but a skeleton of
What was once a wonderland.
Autumn is a dead memory of days gone by.
Here I sleep in my tent of warmth,
While outside
Frost-lace crochets the world.

EMMA FENSOM, *11*


# A Fly Dreams


Explorer,
Adventurer extraordinaire,
Each scrap and every smell
Examined with eye and tongue.
The military brigadier.
Honoured for bravery in the face of danger.
Foods galore
Laid out in a banquet.
The brigadier stands on his six spindly legs.
Silence.
And then he cries,
'We are the flies!
We rule the air!'
And then...meringues, sausages, grapes and bread
Tucked neatly into mouths,
Helped by long and sticky tongues.
The foolhardy flies, noisy in their merrymaking...
Wake up the fruit.
A huge peach,
Not yet touched,
Sprouts eight black matchstick legs,
Two antennae.
And then it sheds its pink fleshy skin.
There it stands,
A huge black spider.
They don't stand a chance;
Flies are dead everywhere.
Some still twitch legs as nerves die.

Most lie still.
The brigadier dares not move
As the spider closes his jaw around the tiny neck.
Snap...
He wakes up,
His antennae searching the air.
There...
His honeycombed eyes focus on the doorway
As he heads towards the kitchen!

IAN LAWLESS, *13*


# The Dream of Persephone


Persephone dreams,
Dreams of a meadow
Where nothing is still,
Nothing is sad or lonely.
A giant multi-coloured spotted quilt –
A patch of picture-book poppies
Sways in the wind.
A stronger breeze blows them
And their petals
Turn into thousands of red butterflies.
A cloud forms,
Blotting out the sun,
Leaving a red light.
But soon it scatters
And just long grasses remain.
Slug trails cover a large stone
Like a child's first drawing.
The trees lining the meadow
Have crows' nests on their tops,
Hair with specks of dirt.
And an apple tree grows ping-pong ball fruit.
A brook runs through this paradise
Like a silver ribbon
Binding it up into reality.

JANE WEAVER, *12*

# 6. THRESHOLDS

*Illustration:* EUGENE COLLINS, *13*

# The Ford

I trot to the ford
On my pony,
Holding my breath
Because I know what happens.
He sees the talking, whispering water
And stops dead,
His legs stiff,
As if holding a heavy weight.
Then, he veers to the left,
His every muscle straining mine.
His hooves chatter on the road,
He rears like a flame,
And lands like spilt water.
Then, upset and shaking,
His feet touch the water,
His legs vibrating like a rubber band.

His neck is tense
And hard, tautly strung.
He leaps,
As if jumping from rooftop to rooftop,
And lands,
And trots shakily on.

CLIFFORD BLACK, *12*


# Starling

A jeweller's skilled hands shaped a small jet stone
That was born an eye.
An eye that now stares, so terror-stricken.
The eye is looking out from a starling's torn feather coat.
The broken china bird limps across the arm of the chair.
And flaps his stiff wings in a last attempt to escape.
He lands.
A dead heap on the floor.

Lost the battle with the closed windows,
And now is battered and bent.
A young bird and yet so old and crooked.

The jet stone eye, so beautifully crafted by the jeweller,
Still stares.

HELEN WALKEY, *13*


## The Truth of a Bullfinch


Last night it happened...
There on the wood painted doorstep
the murderer had left it.
The light orange of its breast
clashed with the colour of the bricks.
It lay with its head slightly flattened
against the concrete.
Cold, dead, no reviving.
Its eyes, closed,
Slits like button holes
in a baby's waistcoat,
and rimmed with an outline of black.
Its feet were cushioned in its stomach.
Its loose plumage blowing
in the wind like sewn-in segments
of feathers from its tail,
divided into five
different colours.
Then, its black helmet, where underneath
its black eyes were hiding.
Its beak, the colour of slightly burnt wood,
thick and ugly.
And its black wings
brought closely together, rolled up
like the ends of two cream horns.
Next was its tail,
a spatula, slightly bent.

And there it was...
propped against the doorway,
unable to venture through the storms and the sunshine,
left in its death.

HILARY FOSTER, *13*


# Fox

The stream falls away steeply,
Not quite a waterfall.
Roots curve over from its crumbling mud banks,
Twisted arches of the Earth's bone.

He sniffs the air, smelling the dripping leaves.
The stream dribbles quickly by,
Weaving and halting
At fallen branches.
Damp rotten twigs
Flake only slightly under his soft weight.
He feels the damp Earth between his toes,
Delicately picking his way through
The scattered pebbles;
Stumbling only once.

Downstream the foundations of a tree
Have been gutted by rain and wind;
And the tree rests across the water,
One sinewy branch hanging, bending against the rush.
He flits up the bank,
His steps flicking brush strokes
On flaking canvas.
He reaches out his paw to the mossy log,
And they go hand in hand.

Cautiously he edges out on to the log;
Tail raised for balance.
One of his first few steps slips
On the thin wet moss.
It starts to rain, heavily;
His fur is drenched, and is stood on end,

Clustered in little spikes.
His tail comes down;
On line with his back, it bristles, the white tip darkening.
The rain washes away his caution,
As he runs lightly across
And up the crumbling, sodden bank,
Off through the trees to the holt,
Churning the wet pine needles,
Leaving the bare earth to the patchy sky.
And through the trees, to his left,
The fiord is painted grey by the rain.

STEPHEN GARDAM, *13*


## The Winter Seashore


Frost nipped at our ears and ankles,
Leaving them pinched pink.
We dodged tiny wet mirrors of water
And our mouths breathed eggs of steam.
Climbing the great bank of sandy shingle was impossible.
Each footstep of sand tumbled down
And took you with it.
Then, at the top of the giant barricade,
The almighty mouth of water
That had swallowed sand and cliffs
And if we were not careful, it would swallow us.
And now as I looked out to sea,
There was no skyline, just a vast palette of murky paint.
We walked, but the wind was so strong
That it blew us into a sidestep,
Then a lunge,
A dislocated pattern.
This wind played games with our minds.
This sea,
Frosted in motion, took us in his hands,
And swallowed us.

EMMA BUCKINGHAM, *12*

# The Journey

The train pulled away,
Another rhythm on the rails returning
The early morning sunlight
As fresh as a new fall of snow
Pure and untouched.
A splinter of sunlight glinted on the window.
Fields wrinkled away from the line,
One looking like velvet,
Tractor marks – brushing it the wrong way.
A deer – playing tag with my eye,
All its limbs
On loose hinges,
Ran into the trees.
Startled rabbits dotted about,
Mistaken for tufts of rotted grass.
Then...the old disused station
Holding many a memory,
Waiting for a new coat of paint
And like an old clock
Waiting to be wound up.
The train shuffled through the countryside
Like a caterpillar.

Until...
Slowly, it slurred to a stop.
My journey's end.
I opened the door
And stepped out
Onto a platform
Buzzing and busy.

HEIDI MASTERS, *13*

# Old Man Cactus

The old man cactus is covered in long snow-white hair
But he has no eyes to see with, no ears to hear with,
And no mouth to speak with.
Yet in his own mind
He knows the world that walks past his window-sill.
For old man cactus is wiser than the trees.
He learnt long ago how to live in the hot yellow deserts
Where no other plants survive.
With great cunning he covered his back in cruel spikes –
No creature could bite him open or drink his blood.
He knew the great heart of the sun
And the long cold stab of the night.
But old man cactus survived them all.
He sat in his dry hot bed
Waiting for someone to come...
And they did in time.
They pulled him from his socket
And put him into a warm moist bed.
From thereon he lived for years and years,
Growing his beard longer and longer.
Happy to sit in the sunshine
And happy to watch the rain fall down past his window-sill.

JOANNE DRAKE, *13*


# Playground

The playground is a Roman Arena
where teachers watch with Caesar's eyes.
The marbles roll like chariot wheels
hitting their opponent
and reaching their goals.
Birds sing in the tree tops,
fanfare their song
with the soldiers.

I run about in the playground
with William, playing 'It';
it's just like the Grand Prix,
dodging here and there like kingfishers.
Then I meet up with Roberta in the kissing corner,
and say, 'Boy, you're ugly!'
She slaps me round the cheek;
it feels like a whip across my face.
The field is a glorious wave of grass and daisies.
We all just relax and talk
as if we are on 'After Dark'.
One slight movement from a bell sends everyone running;
doors burst open,
letting streams flow into the empty spaces of the school.

NIKI HURREN, *12*


## Sports Day


The sound of cheering died,
as the heavy door closed behind me.
I looked up and down the corridor.
No one.
Nothing but the silence.
I shivered...there was something...

I opened the juniors' door
and looked in.
Sun shone through the ivy in the huge windows
and picked out the falling dust showers.
Pencil shavings lay by the bin
and pictures and paintings hung on the wall.
But I saw no one.

The infants' door swung quietly open...
a spade lay discarded in the sandbox
and a curtain flapped in the breeze.
No noises of laughter, chatting or singing.
No one was there,
but the gerbil asleep in his cage.

As I walked down the corridor,
cool, dark air hung about me.
I heard a whistle blow in the distance,
then cheering.
And as I walked out of the door,
someone crossed the finishing line.

SARA WORTS, *12*


## The Old Lady


The day we went bob-a-jobbing
We met her.
She sat there
In a dainty old chair.
She never moved,
Her faint white hands
Perched on the chair
Like two shot birds.
She was wrapped head to foot
In blankets and shawls
As if she was a hermit crab
In her neutral home.

Wrinkles curved over her soft face
As if a snail had left its trail.
She opened her mouth
And mumbled, 'Hello.'
She looked pleased with herself
Like a child who had just
Learnt to write her name.
Her hair –
What was left of it –
Looked like tiny spiders' webs
Knotting all over.

She took my hand
As if to say, 'Come closer.'
She felt my face

As if wondering whether to buy me or not.
She clutched my hand harder,
Then let go.
I sniffed a pricey perfume
Over her clingfilm skin.
Then with a great sigh
She leaned back into her chair.
I knew then, it was time to go.

ROBERT ADCOCK, *10*


## Sat on the Wall


They spent hour after hour,
Day after day,
Year after year
Sat on the wall.
One,
Thin and frail looking.
Long chicken neck
Sprouting up from the faded collar
Of his whipped-up shirt.
His eyes,
Short-sighted slits
Swollen round the edges like pink puffballs,
Lost in the stubby bristle of his face.

The other,
Plump, like a puffed-out cockerel.
His face,
Wrinkled like apple peel
On a compost heap.
Torn nets of burst veins
Knotted in reds and blues
Round his cheek bones,
Overcast by the shadow
Of his flat cap.

They sat on the wall,
Staring in bewilderment at me playing swingball.
Remembering
How once they amused themselves
Throwing pebbles at tin cans.
They sat,
Pondering over the differences
Between their childhood
And mine.

The frail one held tight
To the lead of an old dog,
Which nosed between his legs,
Pining for attention.
The other
Shuffled the dust
With the toe of his boot
And leaned with clasped fingers
On his walking-stick...
For year after year,
Sat on the wall.

Then,
The frail one died.
And I never saw the other again.
The plump one never
Sat on the wall.
It wasn't the same
Without his friend...

LARA MAIR, *12*


## Peace


The cat's bowl,
Cream curdling,
Sits on the doorstep,
Still on that old chipped saucer.
The door creaks as I enter.

Home?
The wallpaper,
Tea stained,
Peels off the wall.
In the kitchen
A tap drips,
Dripping like the blood
From an old friend.
A wife runs to hug me
But I have forgotten what love is.
A window ledge...
With dead flies scattered
Like bullets.
Out of the window
Yellow rape sprawls
Across the fields
Like a never ending marching army.
The church bells sound
In the distance.
But I am lost in my memories
Of the dark trenches
Where the war songs still echo.

KIRSTY PRIESTLEY, *13*

# 7. MINI-BEASTS

*Drawing:* **KELLY WATERS,** *13*

# The Grasshopper

He's been wound up,
then set off,
springing like a mad flea.
His yellow body of patterned plasticine
springs in and out like a trampoline.
His slim grim face
and his cold slit eyes
seem to stare, but not see.
He's the grasshopper.
The wound-up green jet.

HELEN WARD, *11*


# The Fly

The fly is a scurrying maid
humming a tuneless melody as she works,
cleaning the unseen traces of sweetness.
She cleans around an empty mug,
her legs moving like a nimble gymnast
walking the beam.

The maid is a fearless creature,
always entering without being invited,
not afraid to remove rotting food,
her translucent wings fixed to her body,
folded down to make a crocheted shawl.

The maid has lemon-fresh wits,
sharp, sour and bitter.
She walks on my bare arms,
her light legs gently tickling me.
I move my arm, command her to leave,
and she hurries away, only to return
through another door.

The maid spots a spider's web.
The dusty silk threads tempt her,

This web which looks like fishing line,
and has similar purpose:
but to trap a fly, not a thrashing fish.

The maid flies into the line,
and is caught;
her body struggles like a fish on land,
her furry legs splaying in different directions.
Angrily she hums, sounding like water
hissing on a stove.

The maid is exhausted, her shawl is split,
her charring overalls are hung up.
As the angry humming fades
I feel sorry for this maid,
always hurrying, scavenging for food.
Even as her busy life
leaves her.

CAROLINE ENGLISH, *13*


# The Bluebottle


A metallic bubble
Hovers about the room,
Weightless.
Like a stub of blue chalk.
Still and floating.
It settles on my hand,
Licking and caressing my skin, cautiously.
I jerk my hand.
It's gone on its loud frantic flight,
Round the room,
Then it stops dead,
Eyes watching.
Swivelling motionless.
Body glinting purple in the sun,
Like a small diamond.

RHYS HARPER, *12*

# The Truth of a Bluebottle

A thief.
Buzzing away, with greasy butter
Stuck to his back legs.
Escaping death by an inch.
Then again, daringly,
Down on to the bread – the cheese
And once round the sweet sticky glass of orange.
Then, just missing the hanging graveyard.
His friends stuck there, glued down and dead.

He sits, resting on the window sill.
Licking off the tasty, dirty mixture.
Legs quickly flipping,
Up and over his back
Like a twig over an oily puddle.
His big sieve eyes,
Mysterious looking.
Then, with a flit of his delicate wings,
He is off, singing his irritating one-tone song.
Past the window.
Shining like a drip of water caught by the sun.

But this time,
The great slapping swat
Comes straight for him.
Sudden pain
Then he drops
And with a bump, lies stunned on the table top.
An injured soldier not wanting to die.
Sudden panic.
For hours he lies on his back,
Loudly buzzing.
He rocks and slips in a small circle.
Hopeless legs stick up, kicking out in front of him.
Then, at last, he closes his eyes,
The buzzing stops
And tired and hopeless he dies.

THEA SMILEY, *12*

# Worms

A worm comes wriggling
through the earth
as if it's been buried,
its dark purple body
stained by blackberry juice,
lines every little way
as if you could pull it to pieces
like an orange in segments.

Lines move in, out, in, out,
as if it's trying to pump out
blackberry juice.
Veins are grey and look brittle.
Here comes another one.
His head lifts
under a clot of mud.
His one big purple muscle
refuses to move.

Then the body
trickles along the earth...
but now he lies
perfect in my memory,
the stained worm, dead.
The worm earthed –
the blood-clotting movement dead.

LORRAINE DIXON, *12*


# Ants

Jaws like steel,
Jaws like steel clamps.
Legs fixed precariously, three on each side
To the body
Which is joined to the head

Which has water-drop eyes,
And antennae
Moving frantically on invisible looms.
Neck, strong like a crane,
While the body is the engine.

An ant hill is the opposite
Of a bird's nest;
Instead of long winding twigs
An ants' nest has thin,
Long winding tunnels.

The nest is a cow pat
Peppered with an air rifle.
Invisible roots spread down.
And on top they grow like moss.
Inside are unplanned catacombs
Weaving drunkenly,
Often falling, then rising,
Crawling, and at times,
They sleep.

Like man
An ant wants to fly.
Ants with stained glass windows,
Drained from their holy splendour.
Flying ants, like corn being thrashed.
The ant's body is grain
Lifted by husks
Which vibrate in the wind
Propelling the grain forward.
The husks are strained, weary
From flying up and down.
Slowly the husks loosen,
Turning the grain more earthbound
Every flight.
The glass is lost,
Only leaving the lead
Bent and smashed.
The grain lies dormant...

CLIFFORD BLACK, *13*

# The Bee

The bee is...
a seed,
never been planted,
caught in air currents,
forever,
until now.

The bee is planted into my brain,
already growing into my life.
Its body...
a pencil-shaving
curled up
and held together by elastic bands.

The wings are wound up, then released
like aeroplanes won at the funfair.
(sold by the man with a London accent),
but which break on their first flight.
Each wing is made from...
decomposed leaves
half turned into loam
so you can see through them.

Its dance,
unique,
speaks to you...
left, up, right, down.
Dr Dolittle's tango of the night
is finally translated.

ADAM HUGHES, *12*

# Snail

The snail is an old,
wise creature
whose shell was borrowed,

borrowed from an unborn chick
and carved by the snail's
soft, soft body.

The shell, wafer thin
but curled strongly,
almost delicately like a
whip of cream.

Underneath the shell,
a body,
soft with age
with a never-ending supply of moisture.

Two antennae,
upright; soft but
stiff like a flower's stem.

He moves steadily
in his own pace
and leaves a line of silver.
Lengths of fishing line coiled on the ground

In ever decreasing circles.

ROBERT ADCOCK, *11*


# The Autumn Snail


A snail,
a ridged and broken pot
engraved in grime,
budges along my boot
on a juddering mini conveyor-belt,
leaving sticky patches like glue on the black,
determined to get to his home –
a leaf,
but like a huge canvas to him.
His antennae
feel the way, going crazy

like wild and bendy knitting needles
finding the way to a feast
of maggotty apples
left from summer.
He takes a look.
Then Crunch. He engraves the mud
beneath dad's big brutal boot.

HELEN WARD, *12*


## Moth

The Moth is a clumsy overweight snowflake.
Its feather-like antennae sense danger,
Receiving light beams from a high up torch.
Snowflake wings that flap with no sound.
Like an owl in mid-flight...
And the dusty fur coat that will rip at a touch,
Like a piece of brown charred paper.
Six furry legs stolen from a spider,
The nocturnal beast,
Like a flying tiger.
An armoured fighter,
As soft as a raindrop.

RICHARD MUNNINGS, *11*


## Moth

I hang on to any quiet space,
A forgotten creature of the stable,
House or barn.
My wings are not pieces of stiff cardboard,
But beautiful folds of thin gold leaf,
Dusty with age.
I have seen many different sights.

I have heard the most secret of all the secrets,
As I hid, unseen in folds of thorn-torn material,
Or in an undusted corner.
Some people hate me,
Throw me outside...
But I was there in the stable
That Christmas night.
Hidden in folds of thorn-torn material.

LUCY COLLINS, *13*


## The Christmas Spider

The spider is an eye
Watching the world
With eight scaly eyelashes blinking,
Watching, Waiting, Thinking.
It is a black sheep
Legs multiplied by two.
It is a lost shadow
That someone didn't want,
Didn't need.
The spider is a sharp black flint
Cutting its path,
Like a winding knife.
It spins its web –
A story so long,
So sad.
It is...
A black star
Shooting eight ways
Into the air
And the silken thread
It spins is fit to make a robe
For the babe it watches.

EMMA WALKEY, *11*

# 8. CONNECTIONS

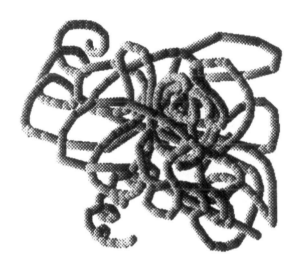

*Illustration:* KIT SWINDALE, *12*

# Letter to a Friend
*(Not to be opened for 50 years)*


Do you remember the pit?
Our hang-out, where we swung
on old matted rope,
out over logs that held our imagination
and shaped our thoughts.
Those logs were wizards and witches;
and the tangled mass of roots
looked like old tennis racquet strings.
But they were sturdy and covered in clay,
moulded over an old man's face.
Do you remember freestyle biking
on my tricycle,
or walking on in the stream?
Each step cracked the ice, leaving footprints
spiked by frost.
Do you remember
sliding down our hill on plastic bags in the snow?
We were dressed for the Arctic
but soon we were hot and slid down the hill
in T-shirts and trousers.
When you read this
you will probably have forgotten me...
I will be an old school friend
and nothing more.
But when you read this
your crocheted web of memories
may hold Emma and Hannah,
the inseparable pair.

HANNAH EDWARDS, *13*

# Friends

We sit on the bank of a ditch.
Two lazy fishermen
In our own lazy way
Throwing stones,
Arms swinging back and forth.

Our boots
Camouflaged in mud,
We are bored.
Minds like blank bullets.
Nothing to talk about.

I kick the water.
It sprays up like a sparkler,
Feasting the banks.
Then something leaps into our minds.
We both start to speak...
'Let's go down the pit,' he says.

Off we go.
A couple of troopers going into battle.
Up on the cliffs –
Last one down does it again!
I jump,
flinging myself off
like a stone from a catapult.
He does it again.

We stagger to the lake,
Wounded soldiers
Suffering from the jump.
Half-way over...
'Let's go home.'
Back we march.
'See ya, Jay.'
'See ya.'

BRYAN HALL, *13*

# Rejected

A ball hits the fired red wall
on which heat is reflected –
stinging my eyes.
A game of girls in a circle,
catching and throwing a ball,
bouncing on hot ground,
like a heart beat,
pounding,
pumping the blood of earth.
I wish I too
could stand side by side
with girls my own age
and play,
while the sun grows smaller but hotter.
Rejected am I
by vicious tongues –
tongues that beat my eyes more than sun.
A tear,
salty sweet,
mingles with sweat and heat,
and is lost,
smudged into my face by the world.

ALEXANDRA WHITNEY, *13*


# The Tree and Uncle George

The tree stands,
Charred as a used match.
Lightning destroyed the mighty oak,
But still there stands a four foot stump
Fifteen years after its fiery fall.

` The death of Uncle George
Is woven into the tree's departure.
The way he used to limp

Through Henham Woods
As the rain slowly seeped
Through his battered raincoat.
His half bald head
Covered in a film of water
That shimmered in the sun
Like an over-glazed pot.

At times the sun
Shone down on his wrinkled face,
Lighting the creases
Like furrows on a field.
And his worn shoes
Were the cut-off roots of the stricken tree,
Wedging him firmly
To the living earth.

MATTHEW BOOLEY, *13*


## Great Uncle: The Death of a Friend

His face was like tired paper,
Creased and dirty;
He did not wear his cap then
As he always used to
And his bald head was so rosy
I could have eaten it.
National Health glasses
Propped on a run-of-the-mill nose
And hooked around
Ears of stamped clay.
His eyes were those of a young lion.
Pawing through the bars of age,
Yearning for hedge and field,
Wood and stream.

We talked about life,
Though he was closer to death.
Close to death...

But still the urge for life.
He needed no charity;
No home would have held him.
Not this lion.
A hospital? Pah!
For the sick.
Weak in body,
His mind took him
Places beyond himself,
Even in his boyhood.

Now only hospital could hold his mind.
And it did.
One week in hospital
Tamed the lion,
Cut hedge and wood,
Ploughed the field...
And he died.

CLIFFORD BLACK, *13*

## Roots

Roots.
Like fragile worms
making their way through the earth,
fat ones that bulldoze through,
so slow but so much power
and ending in white threads of cotton.
Giant
dark trees underground,
the lifeline for all plants,
sucking up water,
a giant pump
which feeds the tree.

A giant underground maze for moles,
Great ropes that spread metres through the soil.
The rough bark that protects the roots,
old person's fingers.

The tree,
unable to stand without roots,
a bicycle without stabilisers.
It is like an iceberg,
the tree,
so little on top,
but so much below.

MICHAEL STAMMERS, *13*


## The Marsh Man

He lay under the bed of reeds
at Oak Field Marsh.
Protected by peat.

Until one day an archaeologist,
who was digging for bones,
stumbled across this human dinosaur,

held together by the thinnest of threads.

Like the shadows of two
skyscrapers

touching tips together
but never colliding
until the thread snaps
and then he's truly
dead in our minds.
Forever.

Until, one day,
we dig again.

PAUL BATLEY, *13*

# The Sparrowhawk

I was only seven
When I saw the sparrowhawk,
Sitting, confused and bewildered
At the back of the cat basket.
He looked around him
As if nothing was right.
He didn't recognise
The criss cross pattern of his wicker cage,
Or the black and white printing
Of the newspapers beneath his feet.
I felt so sorry for him.
I went outside and picked some grass.
'Got something for you to eat,' I said.
And poked it through the bars.
The bird jumped up and lunged at me,
Trying to peck me.
I ran off shouting,
'I only wanted to be friends!'
But I soon came back,
Fascinated by the way he pecked at the cage.
He saw a spider and fell flat
In his hurry to catch it.
I sat for ages just watching
Until it was time for school.
'I'm not going,' I said,
'I've got to look after my friend;
He's hurt his wing.'
I did little work when I got there;
I just sat and thought about my friend.
At home time I ran all the way.
'Where's my friend?' I asked.
'His wing's better,' said mum.
'Where's my friend?' I asked again.
'He's gone back to the other birds.'
I started to cry...
'He didn't even say goodbye.'

JENNIFER WOOLNOUGH, *13*

# Cherry

The first of many goats to come,
Her coat a wiry gloss of brown,
Ears flopped beside her head
And huge pleading eyes of a hazel colour.
Her Roman nose making her look superior...
The mouth that was always chewing
And was passed down to her kids
Who could undo shoe laces, pull buttons off.
Her most outstanding feature was her head,
Constantly butting people playfully.
It was like the waves bumping against a boat.
She was tough and obstinate,
A bully amongst our growing herd.
When milking time came, she would stand, a statue,
Occasionally looking round to check everything was all right.
Then the day came when she fell ill.
She walked around, dejectedly,
A solemn face, set, hard as a stone.
Gradually weaker every day,
No longer the bully of the herd
But a meek and feeble lamb.
She didn't even attempt to butt,
Just lay, a victim of illness.
It got too bad, too painful for her and us to bear.
We had to call the knackers.
It was for her own good.
The men came with their gun.
They weren't even going to take her away
To do the work of the devil.
I ran, trying to escape from her weak face.

Bang!

I cried all of that day.

NAOMI RAVEN, *13*

# She Called It Her Robin

She called it her robin,
And once she took me to see.
All she did
Was outstretch her hand
And sprinkle
Cheese crumbs
On the palms.
She would call softly,
'Robby, Robby.'
Nothing happened at first,
But then,
A rose bush
Sprang to life
As her robin,
Wings vibrating,
Flew from his nest in the roots.

He landed delicately
On her palm.
His breast was brick red,
The edges a musty orange
Fading into the brown of his back.
His eyes shone,
Chips of wet flints
Smoothed round.
His beak was like the tip
Of a rose thorn
As he pecked for the cheese.

She spoke to him soothingly,
Dragging out the vowel sounds,
'Robby, my little Robby,'
The tip of her little finger
Tracing down his back
As she lovingly stroked
Her fickle friend.

LARA MAIR, *12*

# Robin

The Robin is the creep of the class,
with his discoloured hunched back
and his small crocheted head,
which holds his close-set compass-point eyes.
When around people you're a gentleman,
a prince of good manners.
But alone you're a bully, pushing and shoving for food.
You're a prison officer, the one that lets nothing pass your eye.
You think no-one knows
but I saw you through the window.

You have no neck; you're just a lump of clay,
moulded by a three year old,
and burnt in the kiln.
You're a tramp,
living in kettles and old broken boxes.
Your legs are knock-kneed, backwards.
Living on other people's mistakes,
and learning from nothing.
Your song is a war dance
and your red breast says,
This is a warning:
red alert
emergency.

HANNAH EDWARDS, *12*


# The Goldfish...

is a splinter of mineral,
mined by Neptune.
Nothing stirs
in its own narrow world of undisturbed peace.

Its comfort...
reflection.

The duel begins –
a quick bolt from watching eyes
from above,
a challenge with no end.

The goldfish is a sort of...
delicate feather
made from tiny mirrors,
reflecting everything beautiful.
Its eyes look like frog-spawn
with minute tadpoles in the middle.

I feed it. I clean it. And talk to it.
But I get nothing in return...
As if its body is here,
yet its mind is in a coma far, far away.
I wonder if it can hear me.
I get nothing in return
from this delicate splinter of a fish.

ADAM HUGHES, *12*


## The Thought Cat

There was a bowl
Of cream in the kitchen.
Inside my head a cat mewed
And spelt its name 'CAT'
In creamy letters.
The cream was a projector screen
Which enabled me to see the cat.
He was licking his paws and cleaning his face,
Getting ready to JUMP,
JUMP out of my thoughts and into reality.
I looked at the bowl of cream.
There was my cat,
Drinking the cream,
My cat.
I reached out to stroke it.

It leapt out of my reach
And curled up by the fire,
Purred and melted away
Into my memory,
My cat forever.

MARIE FENN, *13*


## The Call of St Francis

Come to me –
And bring me your truths.

Fish,
Swim to me;
Let your fins
Like softened seashells
Hear my call and bring
A lock of my hair,
Turned green by algae,
Sealed in your memory
Of plants and stones,
Forward to the sea of my making.

Bird,
Fly to me;
Let your wings
Feel my call and bring
The snap of your beak,
As sharp as the sound that you heard
When you broke into my world,
Forward to the tree of my making.

Animal,
Run to me.
Rabbit,
Let the spring uncoil and
Leap to me
With bent-back ears

Like ballerina's feet.
Snake,
Crawl to me
On your chess board stomach
And tell me the secrets of the ground.
Lion,
Run to me
With your mane of arrogance
And paws like clover leaves
And share your jungle with me.
Hear my call and bring to me
The space of your desert
Like the palm of my hand;
My sweat,
Your feverish heat.

Walk by my side
Or fly at my shoulder;
Swim at my feet
And give me your souls;
Make me whole with your stories of life
And make yourselves whole with mine.

LEANORA DACK, *13*

# 9. AT RISK

*Drawing:* ANNA ROCHEAD, *12*

# The African Elephant Speaks

There used to be thirty
when I was young;
now there are only five.
The rest are dead;
their mothers carried them for nine years.
They wasted their time.
They're on the mantlepiece now,
well, part of them.
The other part is lying on a pile, rotting.
Some were as young as one year,
their little ears flapping
and their bodies wobbling, caked in mud.
Their eyes were like black diamonds,
fitted in wrinkled rock.

EMMA NEILSON, *11*


# The Rhino

The rhino is a child's model
made out of clay,
the crinkly folds casting shadows
over its rainy day back.
Its big sad eyes stare at you
as if to say, 'Help me.'
His creased eyelids blink
back the tears.

His legs – stubbed-out cigarette ends,
wallow in the mud, making craters
in the soil.
The horn – a huge cornet
of matted hair –
is the jinx of the rhino.
That is all he is hunted for.
And the lead from the bullets
has turned his skin grey.

KIRSTY BUTCHER, *13*

# Highland Ox

I once knew a beast that roamed
In the Highlands;
Its horns were a truncheon,
Big,
Battered.
The matted hair was an orangutang's chest,
Or a half dried wig
Tossed and strewn about.
Its legs were oak stumps,
The rings showing age,
With a dry crust of mud for bark,
Flaky,
Crumbled.
It had the skin of a rhino
And was tough as leather.
It was wild,
Could have known John the Baptist,
The locusts and honey.
He wandered all day,
But never moved,
Chewing the same cud for years,
Worn white.
Until, one day,
Some men parked a landrover on the brow of a hill.
One wielded a shot gun.
Suddenly, a crack!
Doves shot out of a nearby forest;
A dog whimpered half a mile away.
And there was a thud
Of rock,
Clay
And heaving bones.
I never saw him again.

PAUL SPARKES, *13*

# The Hare

The Hare is a messenger
taught by Hermes.
He has speed as a sword,
the elements his shield.

His eyes are ocean depths,
surrounded by a brown ring,
a twisted root,
a mind's eye.

His ears are two golden plates
with a trapped urge for man to hunt.

On his bow back
lies a black stripe, a battle wound
to go with his March madness.

The Hare's whiskers are sensitive to life,
the ultimate defence.
His nose is – just drawn,
and left,
wet,
delicate.

The Hare is created.
It leaps out of infinity
and bounds its way into life.

NICHOLAS KEEGAN, *13*


# Field

I had seen the hare twice that summer.
The sleek ears
Draped back over
Mottled fur.

The first time,
The lean body had leapt
From my view
As quickly as an arrow
Loosed from a bow.
When I saw him again
I lay in the grass,
Unobserved,
Under the oak tree.
He sat upright in the field,
His wary eyes watching.
Glass marbles held between fingertips.

And now the lean body
Spread out like the blanket,
Stained with poppy petals.
The wire, flung to one side,
Knots in a piece of string.
The patches of darkness,
Of death,
Creep over the lifeless body.

I turn my head away.

RACHEL GARDAM, 13


## The Winter Hare

The furious blizzard...
like my brush
flicking water colour
over the finger-smudged canvas.
But there...
    a flash
    a stroke of soft shiny oil.
A hare,
    jumping
    bouncing
    through the slush,

the slush, like
my mixing tray,
wet and sloppy.

The hare runs
into the hedgerow,
the bare bushes
like a flaking frame.
It stops in the
wet damp leaves...

Its little soft nose twitching
like my wet black sponge,
its whiskers like
some of the finest
bristles out of my stiffest brush.

Its bulging eyes are...
like blobs of oil paint
shining and glistening
in the wet winter's light.

Its mouth, a small
smiling mouth,
nibbles at a rotten twig.

Its ears,
two finely cut pieces
off an artist's rag,
frayed and smoothed.

But there it sits,
a beautifully made animal,
frightened,
starved,
with a future of
death.

GAVIN GOODWIN, *12*

# A Shrew

A shrew
is fierce.
A versatile sort of chap
with a long pointed nose,
like a pen nib with a black pimple on the end,
which sniffs its way through pebbles, stones or wire netting –
or gives each obstacle a nudge in a temper.
Its long brows hang over its eyes with a sharp look.
It's like water trickling over pebbles in a stream
as it scurries about.
Just bones,
with a short covering of fur and a long pink tail.
The trap goes.
This shrew was fierce.

ROBERT FILBY, *10*


# Red Squirrel

Leaping as a dash of deep orange inferno!
Delicacy in its dance
over green (damp) limestone, dry stone walls.

In the Lake District I saw it
in a soft peat wood
of steep wet walks.
Overlooking Windermere
on a rainy day,
near an old ruined castle
with tall green pines
– it scuttled up one.

Gnome ears pricked up
with a tuft on the tip
like a sprig of fresh water.
And big globe eyes.

A gush of wind blew drops on our heads.

Swivelling its body,
jumping,
it clutched a nut and chiselled its teeth along the lines
to eat it.
Turned once again
and a tail flew down a hole.

And that's the only time I've ever seen one.

ROBERT FILBY, *12*


# The Barn Owl

The Barn Owl is the Duchess of the woods.
She lifts her wings
As if hitching her skirt to her knees.
Her silk bloomer legs throw her into the air,
And then comes her magical flight...

Her wings beat with grace – and power.
Then...
She glides through the air.
Her X-ray vision scans the ground beneath.

You or I would say that that was just a pebble.
But the owl knows that that pebble is a mouse.
The mouse knows that the Duchess wants her rent,
But, of course, he cannot pay.
So she takes his life.

She stops,
Hovers,
Dives,
And lands on the pebble exactly.
Her cat-like talons pierce the mouse's skin
And now the mouse has paid with his life.

WILLIAM MAIR, *10*

# The Bat

The bat is...
an overgrown owl pellet,
grey fluff and bones,
blowing around in the wind.
Or maybe he is the piece of rag
we gave to our cat,
that he tosses up in the air.
He is a dirty sidekick
sleeping in any hole
planning to kill the king,
together with his lord.
Or maybe only a rodent, cruelly strapped up with silk,
pushed off a cliff,
and told to fly.
At night he is a living cannonball
flying out of his cave at 90 mph
like something out of the circus.
When he hangs motionless as a coathanger,
he is a living insecticide,
eating all the bugs.
But how is he rewarded?
He is outlawed,
framed,
for something he is not.

ALAN SHIELDS, *13*

# Seal

On the sand by the rippling water
his coat gleamed in the moonlight
as if coated in thin silver.
Or had dust fallen from the star overhead?
He slid into the water,
easily,
as if covered in grease.

Oily colours drifted in the waves
and the moon's rays threw lazers
through the night sky.
Webbed paws were his paddles,
racing his clay body away from the hunter.
The star beckoned him on.
And he followed the light once more.

JESSICA BROWN, *12*


## At Dunwich


At Dunwich
You can wander through the forest,
The ground sprinkled with pine needles,
Littered
As the floor of a bird's nest,
The moth-wing prints
Of rabbits' paws
Winding through bushes,
The pine trees
Spearing the sky,
Giant quills
Sucked dry by blotting paper clouds.
Ivy,
Knotting through a barbed wire fence,
That has rubbed off rust
Onto the blistering stems.

At Dunwich
You can shuffle through sand
On the oil clotted beach,
Swelling your head
With the salty smell
Of fresh cod.
Seagulls
Gliding on air currents
As they fly in the wake
Of the fishermen's trawlers.

At Dunwich
You can walk the cliff tops.
Grass,
Bristle cut in tufts
Sprouting out from behind mole hills.
Skeleton trunks
Of dead trees
Lining the path,
As the edge creeps gradually nearer,
Falling prey to the sea.

At Dunwich
You can stand,
Looking at the last gravestone
Eaten by lichen,
Branded by the irons of decay.
A subtle mound
Of darker grass,
Waiting,
Waiting to melt over the cliff
And join other graves,
Lost at sea...

At Dunwich.

LARA MAIR, *12*


## Dunwich

On the corner, there is a walnut tree.
Stretching its gnarled limbs
High,
For the wind to turn its leaves
To face the sea.
To face the sea that didn't used to be;
When the walnut tree had no reason to stretch before the wind.

Now a car park, one or two tufts of rope blowing,
Commands the bottom of the picture,
A picture unframed, wild but tamed.
The new cafe to the right,
Marshy dunes to the left.
But, at the top,
The sea, the sky,
The fishing boats.
Carved, wood splintering,
Lying like a herd of well-fed
But hollow sea cows.
Then the sea.

Grey, tops of the waves just brushed with white,
With the furthest curve of the stony beach
Stuck niggling in one corner
With the crumbling cliffs
A line of formless village elders;
Elders of the village of Britain
Sat in a never-ending war council against the sea.
And losing the cold war.

STEPHEN GARDAM, *13*

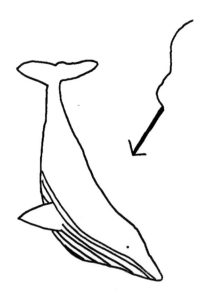

*Drawing:* ANNA ROCHEAD, *12*